Pushing North

Tame the Mind, Savor the Journey

Trey Free

AKA Early Riser

ISBN: 9798531219220

DEDICATION

This book is dedicated to all those with dreams on the horizon. To those who are getting closer to throwing their hat into the ring of life. To those who realize life is meant to be lived as a journey, not confined to a world of safety and comfort. Life is now . . . go find yours!

CONTENTS

	Acknowledgments	i
	Preface	1
	Introduction	4
1	Framing the Challenge We Face	12
2	The Divided Mind	21
3	The Rider	33
4	The Elephant	43
5	The Path	55
6	Perceptions	66
7	The Danger of Expectations	82
8	Fear and Clinging	93
9	Our Behavior Becomes Our Biggest Obstacle	110
10	Our Habits and Change	123
11	Sleep is Our Superpower	144
12	Building the Mental Bulwarks	158
13	The Power of Gratitude	169
14	The Alter Ego Effect	181
15	Trail Time is NOT Matrix Time	191
16	Breathe	204
17	The Nature of it All	215
	About the Author	221
	References	222

ACKNOWLEDGMENTS

I want to take a moment and thank my wife for, once again, affording me the opportunity to live in local coffee shops while I wrote another book. She also spent her precious time editing and providing feedback on the thoughts contained in these pages. She is the one who keeps me oriented to my true north and prevents me from straying too far off course. She also offers me the latitude to experience new arenas where I can push my boundaries of what is mentally and physically possible. You just can't ask for any more than that! We all need a rock in our lives, and I am so lucky she is mine!

Preface

Those who say it can't be done should not interrupt those doing it.

Chinese Proverb

I feel it's important to reveal why this book was written, and why it was written by me. It's also important to recognize that I am not some ultra-accomplished, triple crown-wielding thru-hiker that has 10,000 miles of hiking under my belt. I've never taken one step on trails like the Pacific Crest Trail or the Continental Divide Trail. I haven't found the courage to uproot my Matrix life, to live a minimalist lifestyle, to pack everything I own inside a 35-liter backpack, to devote the rest of my days chasing those expansive mountain views, or to put one foot in front of the other on these long-distance trails year after year.

On the flip side, I've had experiences that afforded me unique perspectives on the mental challenges we face as humans. I'm a guy who has spent his entire adult life doing things only a small percentage of humans can do. I devoted 21 years to serving as a special operations forces (SOF) operator. A guy who dealt with daily physical and mental challenges since I was 18. Even after I retired from the military in 2010, I continued working inside one of the most elite SOF units in the world. I have watched the most badass humans on the planet perform at levels I wouldn't have guessed possible if I didn't witness it with my own eyes.

That was the foundation that underpinned my life as I entered the long-distance hiking community in 2017. I needed to put myself back inside the arena to see if my mind could handle the stress of the journey. After four years and 3,000 miles on trail, I discovered that the foundation of a successful long-distance hiker and the foundation of a SOF operator overlap significantly.

With my background in mind, let's shift the focus to you—the reader. To obtain maximum benefit from this book, I hope you will read each concept and translate it into your own context. You might be like me, or you might be completely different, but either way, this book will help you achieve your goals if you apply the concepts correctly. Why? Because we will examine the parts of us that are below the surface. We will dive below our personalities and look at how our biology can change our outcomes. Our goal is to understand how to manage the parts of our minds and bodies that we can control. This focus on our biology should serve as a framework to help us achieve our goals, whether on trail or in life.

Hear this clearly, this book is not just for hikers. It's for anyone undertaking a long-duration journey where the mind will inject itself as the biggest obstacle in our path. It could be during a military deployment, running an ultramarathon, attending a sports training camp, enduring an assessment and selection course for special operations, entering a police or military training academy, grappling with a large project at work, or any other journey where our minds become the largest hurdle on the way to our goals. Therefore, anytime I use the words "thru-hike," or other hiking vernacular, please replace it with whatever endeavor you find yourself on in life. I think you'll discover that these concepts will help you achieve whatever goals are on your horizon.

My meaning and purpose are simple: I want to help you finish what you start. I want you to reach the far terminus of your journey successfully. I want you to experience the magic and growth that awaits you along the path. If I can help one person achieve their dream, then all of this will be worth it. Enough "prefacing" . . . Let's GO!

Introduction

Twenty years from now you will be more disappointed by the things you didn't do than by the ones you did do. So, throw off the bowlines! Sail away from safe harbor. Catch the trade winds in your sails. Explore. Dream. Discover!

Mark Twain

People love the thought of breaking the shackles of their Matrix life and going for a long-distance hike. I do too. There is something primal about strapping on a pack filled with only the necessities and going on a long walk. I think it's coded deep inside our DNA. I assume it's part of the reason you bought this book. It's also the reason the mountains keep calling you to their soil. We were meant to be in nature, not confined to the safety and comfort of our Matrix dwellings.

Hiking seems to be a perfect means to create a union between nature and the human soul. It provides the opportunity to feel the leaves crunching beneath our feet, to see views that send chills to the depths of our being, to smell the fresh mountain air as the cool breeze washes over us, to hear the joy-filled birds singing their springtime serenades, and to watch the universe paint it all on its canvas without a seam to be found. Hiking allows us to experience ourselves in a way that is hidden inside our Matrix lives. I feel it's one of the purest ways to uncover the true meaning behind this experience we call life.

There are many ways to hike the world's trail systems, but in my humble opinion, one method rises above them all. To be honest, I have never enjoyed day hiking or short out-and-back overnighters. There seems to be a loss of true adventure when I only have a day or two on trail. Worse yet, for me anyway, is to hike a few miles up a trail only to turn around and hike those same miles back to my car. Nope. I find no desire for these short hikes. Maybe the biggest reason is that I still have Matrix thoughts flooding my system during these brief strolls. There is a certain amount of time required to purge these thoughts from my mental system, and these short hikes just can't get it done. I guess it's a good option for those who can't unplug from the Matrix long enough to do a long-distance hike, but it's just not my favorite way to enjoy a trail.

I need the feeling I get when someone drops me off at the southern terminus and there is nothing between me and my distant goal but hundreds or, better yet, thousands of miles of trail. I need to feel the anticipation that the journey will test me to my core. I need to see the mileage sign three weeks into my hike that says I still have 1,972 miles to go. I need to witness winter slowly transforming into spring as I saunter at two miles an hour through nature's wonderland. I need to observe the landscape transforming from mountainous peaks to expansive valley scenes where people are living a simpler life. I need to feel the pain in my lower extremities after the trail collects its tax for the day. I need to feel the exhilaration of making it to the 1,000-mile mark only to realize I'm not even at the halfway point yet. I need to feel those rocks in my hands as I climb up the side of that gorgeous mountain dubbed Katahdin that stands so majestically against Maine's central skyline. I need to feel that cold, worn, wooden sign pressed against my lips as I reach the end of the most incredible journey one could envision.

Those are just a few pieces of the journey I became addicted to when I thru-hiked the AT in 2017. For me, a thru-hike is the only way to garner the soul-cleansing properties a long-distance trail can provide. It's the truest battle between mind and body, and the trail is but a simple stage.

Deciding to thru-hike a long-distance trail might be the biggest life-changing decision a human can make for themselves. However, most up-and-coming hikers fail to realize there is an art to long-distance hiking that isn't obvious until you experience it. It's more than buying some gear, strapping on some shoes, and heading up the trail. Anybody can do that. The art comes from learning how to set small, achievable goals, controlling what's inside our span of control, letting go of the things that aren't, attuning the mind to the environment surrounding us, and squeezing every ounce of fulfillment and joy from the experience as possible. It's about learning to adapt to this different way of living and letting go of the fear and clinging that plagues us inside our Matrix lives.

But here's the secret most don't realize or talk about in the public sphere: a thru-hike only provides maximum transformation if we are willing to stay on trail long enough to receive the lessons. I believe the more people that transform themselves through something as challenging as a thru-hike, the more people we have helping us transform the world. It's a way to help people escape from the Matrix and find the deeper meaning hidden below their surface. Once this discovery happens, I'm hopeful it will guide each of us to the ultimate truth of why we are here. With truth comes action, therefore, the more people we can arouse through awareness, the more people we have helping guide others to their awakening as well.

Hiking a long-distance trail is one of the hardest and most rewarding journeys a human can experience. This book will underline how our thoughts and behaviors are controlled by some deep-seated ancient hardware and emerging software that is still plagued with a few bugs. With this awareness, we can gain more influence over our experience and achieve a deeper sense of fulfillment along the way.

Let's use a metaphor to drive this point home. Imagine you are the experienced pilot of a small, single-engine airplane and you are climbing into the cockpit for your one-thousandth flight. How comfortable should you be with the controls in the cockpit? After a thousand flights, I argue you would be so comfortable that you are pushing buttons, pulling levers, reading gauges, and adjusting handles without having to put much focus on it. This is no different from when we climb into our cars after work and drive to our homes. We climb in, start the car, adjust the transmission, push the gas, and follow the rules of the road . . . all without having to place much mental focus on any of it.

Now, imagine you find a manual underneath the cockpit seat that you have never seen before. You open it and read the first few pages. The book describes a control box located in a secret compartment in the back of the plane. When placed in the cockpit and plugged into an outlet underneath the dashboard, the controls in this box can help adjust specific parts of the engine to reduce internal friction and increase power. The box also provides a new gauge to help build more awareness of the aircraft itself. This gauge displays where the most friction is occurring on the surfaces of the airframe and allows you to make adjustments to reduce the resistance. This reduction in friction will increase airspeed, burn less fuel, and decrease the cumulative stress on both the engine and the airframe. Once you realize what this control box can do for you, would you use it? It's a no-brainer, right? Now let's bring the cockpit analogy back home to you.

Your "cockpit" is the comfortable space in your mind. It's analogous to the cockpit you climbed into before you found the new manual. You are running on the pre-recorded scripts you have created through a lifetime of repetition and experience. The thoughts and decisions that make it into your aware mind are just headlines derived from the countless processes taking place inside the unconscious mind. We are acting out our daily lives with little awareness or focus on what is happening below the surface of our mental conditioning. This often plays out as drama, boredom, anxiety, fear, clinging, and a never-ending sense that we are waiting for something. These scripts keep us erecting our protective walls to ensure we are always safe and comfortable. All of this takes place and feels like normality . . . but it's not normal at all.

This explains why we desire to change things in our lives but can't break free of the mental anchors controlling our behaviors. Our scripts keep us searching for safety and comfort, not novel experiences that help us grow. That's why creating new habits is so freaking difficult. New healthy habits feel bad in the early stages but pay off in the long run (think eating healthy, exercising, or learning to play the piano). This early friction makes many of us quit before the habit takes hold. Bad habits often provide instant gratification early but lead to negative outcomes over the long haul (think eating doughnuts, binge-watching Netflix, or drinking too much alcohol). That's why bad habits and addictions are so pervasive in our culture . . . they feel good initially and our biological systems keep us seeking more of those pleasurable experiences.

What this book represents is the manual you found underneath the cockpit seat, and the control panel you plugged into the plane. This book will give you agency over parts of your mind that are outside of your awareness at the moment. If we can gain some control over the things that disrupt our fulfillment, we can create an experience on trail that is absent of the nagging fears, doubts, misery, and suffering that accompanies our mind's script of "seek safety and comfort at all costs." If we can learn to control the accessible systems inside our mind and quit worrying about things outside of our control, we can create an environment of contentment . . . regardless of what is happening around us. Our brains can keep adapting throughout our life, but most of us need the proverbial manual hiding under the seat to nudge our adaptation in a positive direction.

The human brain is extremely malleable until the age of 25. This means it can modify itself in response to an experience.[1] This neuroplasticity—a scientific term for the malleable brain—enables the human to learn quickly from experience and adjust itself to meet the needs of its environment. In simpler terms, the brain is wiring itself during the early years of your life (think wiring a new house before the drywall is hung) and then executing those functions for the rest of your life (think how you use the light switches and outlets but don't have easy access to the wires and junction boxes inside the walls). Therefore, it's much easier to learn new skills like foreign languages and calculus as a teenager than as a 40-year-old. The teenager's wiring can still be accessed and adjusted easily while the 40-year-old's wiring is much harder to access because we have covered the walls with drywall, paint, caulk, and pictures.

What does this mean for those aspiring to be a long-distance hiker? Well, the first thing it explains is a phenomenon I have noticed both on trail and social media surrounding long-distance hiking. Younger hikers (those in the age group 18 to 25) are rarely involved in discussions about the mental challenges of long-distance hiking. There are countless reasons this may be true, but when we realize this age group is still in the phase of maximal neuroplasticity, it's easy to conceive why they can adapt quickly to trail life and aren't as concerned about it as us older folks. So, it makes sense they don't place their focus on the mental side of hiking. Hopefully, this book can reach some of the younger generation hikers and help them accomplish whatever goal is on their horizon.

For us older hikers, the changes still occur, just not as fast. We are forced to tear down many of our habituated processes that seem to serve us well in our Matrix life but cause friction in our trail life. In our house analogy, those younger than 26 can simply access their wiring and make some quick changes while us older folks must tear down the drywall and try to figure out which wires need to be adjusted. This adaptation period often feels like friction and takes more time than many are willing to endure.

For those of us who haven't seen the good side of 26 for a few years (or decades like me), trail life may require we spend more time adjusting our mental processes (things like our habits, emotional reactions, and belief systems). Tweaking these processes will increase our adaptation ability on the trail. However, if I asked each aspiring long-distance hiker how much time they spent on gear purchases and preparation, compared to the time spent preparing their mind, I am 100 percent certain the stats would overwhelmingly favor gear prep over mental prep. But the real question we need to tackle is, Why?

Why do we know that the mental struggle will be the toughest part of the journey, yet we do the least towards strengthening our minds before our hike? It would be like saying I am going to drive across the U.S. in my car, but only fill my engine with 10 percent of the oil it needs to function effectively. Instead of ensuring the most important part of my car is primed for the journey, I spend the lion's share of my time getting new tires, new windshield wipers, and ensuring the car is spotless before I leave. All of these items are worthless when the engine seizes from a lack of oil. In parallel, the time spent on our hiking equipment proves worthless when our mind decides it's time to quit. We MUST learn how to strengthen our minds so we can adapt more quickly and efficiently once our long-distance journey begins.

That's the gap this book will help fill. It's complementary to previous works on the mental side of long-distance hiking, but we will dive a little deeper underneath the hood to reveal why our mental struggle happens in the first place. If we can gain awareness of why these struggles happen, then we can learn to use some basic strategies to decrease the mental chaos and increase our forward momentum.

As we get ready to move into the main sections of the book, it's important to understand that we are in control of our mental space. However, most of us have lost touch with this. Throughout our life, we have constructed a plethora of stories, thoughts, and conditioned processes that often manifest as chaos when times get hard. Therefore, everything we're going to talk about in this book boils down to one simple fact: if we understand that we're the ones who created this mental chaos, we're also the ones that can tear it down.

I want this book to help people achieve their long-distance hiking goals. I want to provide some tools to prevent you from being the 75 percent of hikers that never reach their far terminus. Strap in and let me guide you towards a place of mental fortitude. Let me provide some tools that can reallocate mental capacity when those difficult moments hit. This is about you making it deep into your journey, where true growth happens. This is about discovering the hidden you underneath the fear and clinging inside your Matrix life. As Mark Twain urged in the epigraph: it's time to "...throw off the bowlines! Sail away from the safe harbor. Catch the trade winds in your sails. Explore. Dream. Discover!"

Chapter One
Framing the Challenge We Face

We are healed of a suffering only by experiencing it to the full.

Marcel Proust

2,200 miles. Let that number sink in for a moment. It seems like an absurd number of miles to consider walking for any human, but thousands of people dream of it every single year.

So how far is 2,200 miles? Let me ask you a question to add some perspective. If you started in Atlanta and walked due west towards San Diego, where do you think 2,200 miles would place you? If you were like me, I assumed 2,200 miles would drop me somewhere in either New Mexico or Arizona. Nope. When walking due west from Atlanta, you will hit the Pacific Ocean around the 2,150-mile mark. To reach 2,200, you must swim an additional 50ish miles into the Pacific Ocean to reach your destination.

This realization blew me away. Not because of the sheer distance, but because the 2,200 miles on the Appalachian Trail (AT for short) routes you, it seems, over every piece of elevation the designers could gain access to. Those 2,200 miles are undeniably brutal on the human body and anyone that attempts a thru-hike of this trail will require a physical output that equals climbing and descending Mount Everest 16 times. A physical output that most can't fathom until smacked in the face with it. So, again, 2,200 miles . . . let that sink in.

Whatever long-distance trail or journey you choose will have its own difficulties that will challenge every single person. The Pacific Crest Trail (PCT) and the Continental Divide Trail (CDT) have large sections of desert to contend with. They also have deep snow in many areas that hikers must navigate as well. The PCT is roughly 2,650 miles in length, while the CDT is approximately 3,100 miles from end to end. Although they don't share the AT's overall elevation gain and loss, they are more remote and don't offer the massive support system the AT enjoys since it's so close to civilization. It doesn't matter which trail you choose, the journey will test you to your limits both mentally and physically. I talk about the AT in this book because it is my lived experience, but these lessons transfer to any long-distance journey you will undertake.

What did my body feel like the day after I reached the summit of Mount Katahdin (the northern terminus of the AT in Maine)? To be honest, it was wrecked. I woke up in my hotel room in Bangor, Maine and could barely walk to the bathroom because my knees and many other joints were locking up and aching terribly. I found this odd though. For the last 113 days, I could wake up and crush miles like a man possessed, but as soon as my mind realized I was finished with the agreed-upon journey, my body started locking up on me. A switch seemed to have flipped in my nervous system that triggered the response of "Hey bro, the threat is over, time to shut down and heal." When we talk about downstream effects later in the book, think back to this example. What I was experiencing at the end of my hike were all the downstream effects of my choices and decisions from the last 113 days on trail.

This pain would stick around in some level of intensity for several months. My knees did not fully recover until September—almost four months after I finished my hike. As an avid fitness enthusiast, I started working out again several days after my summit, but the exercises I could do were extremely limited because of my body's wrecked state. I tried to run, but my fast-twitch muscles seemed non-existent. I never really like to run but not being able to run was shocking to me. I guess walking five million steps over countless mountains will do that to you.

I suffered numerous injuries and a severe illness that plagued portions of my journey. I twisted my right knee several times, injured my right ankle during a fall, somehow acquired bursitis in my left elbow, and caught the dreaded norovirus during the most extreme cold temperatures I would experience during my hike.

As I glance back at what I just wrote, I am not sure I painted an appropriate picture of how mentally challenging walking 20 to 25 miles a day over mountains can be when handicapped by pain, sickness, and extreme weather. Like the time I was throwing up violently in zero-degree temperatures and had to hike 48 miles over the next two days to reach the next trail town. I also remember being six miles short of the Mahoosuc Notch in Maine—noted to be the hardest mile on the entire trail—and watching my left foot slide down a muddy embankment while my right foot stayed firmly planted. By the time I fell to the ground, my right foot was located somewhere behind my back and I torqued my right knee to the point that something popped loud enough to hear. That was the second time a fall exacted its toll on my right knee, and this time I thought I might have to be airlifted out of this remote area of trail. But I stood back up, wiped as much mud off me as possible, and continued my hike despite the pain the fall created. Again, this trail wrecked my body in ways that words will not describe in proper detail, but ask any AT thru-hiker and you will hear similar stories from them as well.

But here is the kicker to all of this . . . the physical side of the challenge is rarely considered the hardest part of a long-distance hike. In fact, if I had to assign a percentage to the physical struggle when compared to the mental challenges, I would give it a scant 15 percent out of 100. (Honestly, that may be a bit overweighted now that I think about it.) The rest of the balance rests solely in the corner of the mental difficulty. I quickly learned that although it was uber-challenging to hike up and down the never-ending mountains, the physical difficulties paled in comparison to being inside my head for 10 to 12 hours a day. I would argue that very few humans have put themselves in situations where they are alone with their minds in such a challenging environment . . . for weeks and months on end.

If you want to know why there is such a high failure rate on these long-distance journeys, I argue it's because most of us aren't prepared to endure this level of introspection for such an extended period. Especially in our culture of information overload that ensures our mental bandwidth is occupied most of our waking hours. Humans have acquired a taste for instant gratification that just doesn't exist on trail. No matter how fast you want to get to your destination, no fast-forward button will make your miles go any faster. We are relegated to an average speed of 2 miles an hour on trail and that is a hard adaptation for most of us when we begin our hike.

Adaptation to trail life is much harder than most expect. Why? Because in our Matrix lives, we seek comfort and safety 24/7/365. It's what nature wired our brains to do. Thinking we can simply step out on the trail for 4 to 7 months and shut down all the mental processes, desires, and attachments we have been clinging to our entire life is just not feasible for most of us. We are too wrapped up in the chaos, and when we separate ourselves from it, our mind creates a level of suffering many can't endure. It incites fear, anxiety, and suffering in hopes we hang up the journey and return home to the safety and comfort it's used to.

It's funny really. Many of us dream about getting away from it all. We dream of quitting our jobs, surrounding ourselves in nature, putting what we need to survive in a backpack, and leaving our normal life behind as we follow those beautiful white blazes to Maine. But reality sets in fairly quickly. Some of us get a few days of pleasant weather at the beginning, which may delay our mental demons from finding us during the first week. Others get slammed early with cold, ice, wind, and rain which offers a quick roundhouse to the mental chin and summons the mental demons immediately. Added to the mix, the first 30 miles of the AT in Georgia are extremely tough for a large majority of new hikers. By the time many get to the 30-mile mark at Neel Gap—the first substantial road crossing with a great outfitter and hiker hostel—they can't imagine having to endure hiking that same distance 72 more times to reach Katahdin. As hikers get the taste of normalcy at Neel Gap (usually in the form of a hot pizza, laundry, and maybe a shower), they often become overwhelmed by the thought of submitting themselves to 2,170 more miles of suffering.

Let me be as clear as possible before we move any further. Any long-distance hike, especially for those who are not prepared physically, can create extreme suffering. Many hikers experience it during those first 30 miles and long for their chaotic lives back inside the Matrix. Why suffer out here in this unfamiliar environment when I can just go back home and suffer in the comfort and familiarity of my house?

Others find the courage to swap out pieces of their heavier gear with lighter options at Neel Gap and keep pushing north. Unfortunately, only 25 out of 100 hikers figure out a way to convince themselves to keep pushing to the summit of Katahdin. Only 25 percent kiss that infamous sign that marks the northern terminus . . . 2,200 miles from where they started. The fundamental question we should all be asking is, Why? Why do so many choose to get off the trail while so few persevere the entire 2,200 miles? It was their dream . . . until it got hard.

Many thought they would find peace and serenity inside an environment of nature and mountains, but quickly realize that suffering overrides the positive emotions trying to bubble to the surface. Again, that begs the question, Why? Why, when things get difficult, do we latch onto suffering so naturally and lose our ability to see the upside in each moment? What draws our mind to see the negative problems surrounding us instead of the beauty we are surrounded by?

One could argue, only one in four hikers discover how to ensure the positives outweigh the suffering. Others may have an uncanny ability to endure suffering and keep pushing forward (I place myself in this camp for the majority of my hike). However, most humans have a hard time fighting the emotions that are ignited when they experience suffering, and they can't comprehend what is happening inside them. This disconnect often leads down the path of quitting, but when asked why, most can't find the words to explain it effectively.

What's interesting to me is the fact that very few hikers that get off trail ever admit, "I just couldn't do it mentally." Maybe we can write it off to human nature's love for crafting narratives to explain away our actions. A common narrative many create revolves around a medical issue they are suffering with—usually some sort of knee, ankle, or foot pain. Their minds often take this discomfort and create a narrative of "Be worried, you may do permanent damage if you keep going" in their heads. When the small percentage of hikers that have accomplished a thru-hike of the AT hear these reasons from hikers only 30 to 300 miles into their journey, most will shake their heads and bite their tongues. Why? Because every one of them had comparable (or worse) pain and overuse injuries during their hike, especially in the early stages when their body was still adapting to trail life. They had to push the pain aside and keep pushing north, day after day.

Bodily pain is a simple reality on a journey of this magnitude. There is no escaping it, and although I was in incredible shape when I started my hike, by the time I reached the Top of Georgia Hostel at mile 70, my kneecaps felt like they were going to shoot off my legs if I hiked down one more descent. I had some mental doubts creeping in that left me wondering if I could keep this up to Katahdin. However, I knew that every successful thru-hiker before me must have faced similar physical pains early in their hikes and they still made it to Katahdin. Therefore, I kept repeating the mantra in my head, "If they could make it, then I damn sure can make it."

What has become painfully obvious is that most hikers who end their hikes early aren't suffering from major injuries that may cause long-term damage. No, most hikers decide to end their hikes because they can't adapt mentally to such an unfamiliar environment outside of their Matrix lives. What they failed to realize is that every single hiker experiences the same type of suffering. It's simply a tax the trail collects from all of us and there's no avoiding it.

That's why I wanted to write this book. I want to enable more hikers to prepare for their upcoming mental challenges and help them adapt to the demands of the trail more effectively. I want as many hikers as possible to experience the same type of moment I had when I reached that monumental sign on top of Katahdin—regardless of what your goal may be for your specific journey. You see, it wasn't climbing that last mountain or kissing that sign that made that moment so freaking special. It was the convergence of the thousands of hours I spent inside my head battling the mental demons that kept telling me it's OK to quit and go back home. The demons that kept nudging me to let go of this journey and return to my Matrix life of safety and comfort. The fact that I withstood those attacks and still made it to the end is what made it so memorable, and that's what I want to help each of you accomplish as well. This reminds me of a powerful quote I read by author Steve Goodier the other day:

> Those who overcome great challenges will be changed, and often in unexpected ways. For our struggles enter our lives as unwelcome guests, but they bring valuable gifts. And once the pain subsides, the gifts remain. These gifts are life's true treasures, bought at a great price, but cannot be acquired in any other way.

I would also be remiss if I didn't mention that I am standing on the shoulders of giants as I offer my opinions in this book. If you haven't read books like *Appalachian Trials* by Zach Davis, make sure you read it right after this one. To me, these books are not in competition with each other. In fact, I would argue just the opposite. I think these books are trying to cover a wide gamut of mentally challenging situations, hoping a tip or technique will land positively on the reader and help them navigate an obstacle successfully. Many of my thoughts overlap with Zach's, and many will be novel concepts you have never considered. Regardless, my aspiration is to help you achieve your long-distance goal with less suffering and more fulfillment along the way.

We will achieve this by placing our crosshairs on the one common obstacle every hiker will face repetitively—our human mind. It's only when we have a foundational understanding of how our mind works that we can step outside of our conditioned thought patterns. Only then can we interrupt the inaccurate stories our mind creates when we face situations that are unfamiliar and uncomfortable. My goal is to give you a basic understanding of what is happening in your mind during your experience. I want to help you prepare more effectively for your journey so you can suppress the mental demons when they find you.

We will also gain an understanding of the conditioned mental processes that guide our behavior. If we gain awareness, we can interrupt their destructive nature inside our mental space. Our behavior is very predictable. If we show up on trail with the exact person we are in the Matrix, we can predict the same suffering we face in our normal lives will manifest on our hike. Preventing this takes focused effort and the willingness to let go of habits that no longer serve us. It also requires adopting new habits that increase our ability to experience fulfillment on our journeys.

Most of us don't realize the levels of suffering we experience because it has become our normality. We simply call it "reality." But what has become hidden from humanity is the fact that we are in control of our perceptions of the world around us. It's how we are perceiving the events of the world that create the suffering, not the events themselves. By understanding why we have a bias to see much of the world as negative problems needing to be solved, we can flip the script on our mind and tune it towards positivity and gratefulness for our experiences. Instead of allowing our energy to be depleted by our unconscious negative triggers, we can focus our intention on the bright spots and use them as wind for our sails.

Let's all agree right now to go all in because these concepts, theories, and lessons can apply to every human reading this. Once we learn to adjust the parts of us we control, we begin playing a different game altogether. We will no longer find ourselves relegated to being unconscious passengers on this journey we call life. Instead, we become the captain of our journey and create a positive experience that will transform us forever.

Chapter Two
The Divided Mind

Reality is created by the mind; we can change our reality by changing our mind.

Plato

All long-distance hikers experience it. When we know what the right answer is, but we just can't make our actions match our thoughts. We want to wake up early to hike more miles, but instead, we smash the snooze button and curl back up under our quilt. We do anything to avoid facing the cold air awaiting us in our tent.

We tell ourselves that we won't push our body past its breaking point, yet we convince ourselves to skip the next town stop and hike our sixth 25-mile day in a row. Despite our sore knees, our aching feet, and our exhausted mind, we keep pushing relentlessly towards our goal.

Our hiking budget is tight and won't allow us to spend but a few nights in a hotel during our long journey. However, in our first town stop, we call the front desk and extend our hotel stay one more night because of the slight chance of rain later this afternoon. Our fear of being uncomfortable drives our short-term decisions and ignores the long-term consequences.

We stand on the porch of a warm hiker hostel at five o'clock in the morning and choose to hike north in the coldest weather to hit Virginia in decades. We would come down with norovirus 12 hours later and suffer immeasurably for our decision to hike in the treacherous artic conditions. We could have simply gone back inside the hostel and waited one more day, but we convinced ourselves we must keep pushing if we want to make our goal in time.

We wake up to a leaking tent and a soaked sleeping bag and decide right then to quit our thru-hike, even though we promised ourselves we would not quit on a bad day.

But why? Why do we often know the best answer in our heads, but take a path that often contradicts our values and goals? Why do we let our finances take a hit just because we see a little rain in the forecast? On the flip side, why do we avoid that gut feeling telling us to slow down and stop the incessant worry about rushing towards our goal? Why do we ignore the voice telling us it's okay to spend one more day in town to avoid the danger of hiking in frigid temperatures? How can we make a contract with ourselves to not quit on a bad day, but then find ourselves on a plane heading home mere hours after quitting on a bad day?

None of these scenarios would surprise any experienced long-distance hiker. I would bet a paycheck that every accomplished thru-hiker has faced many of these same challenges during their journeys. Their ability to fight through all their bad decisions, lazy mornings, hard days, rainy afternoons, and near mental breakdowns are the reasons they climbed atop that wooden sign on Katahdin (or insert your terminus here) and raised their hands in victory. They were able to synch several components inside their minds to achieve their intended goal of hiking 2,200 miles. In doing so, they reaped the true magic that awaits everyone during these journeys, yet most aren't willing to endure the suffering to experience this growth.

That is the goal I want to help everyone achieve, and it's why this book is so important to me. If you have ever watched my videos on YouTube, then you know I have a desire to help everyone serious about reaching a long-distance goal. But to get there, we need to gain an appreciation for the main obstacle all hikers will face on trail. It's not the relentless terrain, the extreme weather, the hordes of insects, the swollen water crossings, the dwindling bank accounts, the dry water sources, the steep climbs, or the butt chafing that hurts with every little movement. No, the biggest obstacle on trail is our chaotic minds.

The experience a hiker enjoys on a long-distance trail is created by a merger of biology, chemistry, physiology, psychology, automatic impulses, past experiences, existing mental conditioning, moral filters, cognitive biases, perceptions, learned knowledge and behavior, and many other pieces that amalgamate to create what we commonly refer to as our reality. For this book, we will stay mostly centered on the biology and psychology of these long-distance journeys, but we must keep in mind that all these pieces of our structure are working to produce the reality we experience. Unless you are like me and like to geek out on the details of "how things work in the brain," these discussions can quickly devolve into words and phrases that eventually sound like blah, blah, blah.

However, before we can get to the tactical "how-to" advice, we must gain a shallow comprehension of how our minds are controlling our experience. This knowledge will not only help us apply some of the simple solutions ubiquitous in the hiking community—never quit on a bad day, start slow in the beginning, smiles before miles, stop to smell the roses—but will also provide the awareness of why our minds create the problems in the first place. If we can understand the root cause, then our ability to apply effective solutions should increase dramatically.

Your Conscious Mind Only Sees The Headlines

If I told you that the only thing we are perceiving in our mind is equivalent to simple news headlines, would you believe me? In other words, when we experience our thoughts and decisions, we are only observing the results from the countless processes our brain had to complete to create the specific thought. In typical human fashion, our conscious mind makes us feel like we're the ones who drove our car down the path to create these thoughts. However, as neuroscientist David Eagleman put it in his book *Incognito,* "The conscious mind is not at the center of the action in the brain; instead, it's far out on a distant edge, hearing but whispers of the activity."

In simpler terms, your conscious awareness is at the mercy of the way you have conditioned your mind throughout your life. For example, if you dislike being cold because you don't like being uncomfortable, your brain will process the sensory data from your environment and send only the headline to your conscious awareness as, "Don't get up yet, this sleeping bag is very warm and the temperature in your tent is frigid." You didn't have to sit there and compute all the factors of why you shouldn't get out of your sleeping bag, your brain did all of that for you. All you needed was the headline, and unless you have a method to overwrite these headlines, your unconscious brain will keep you living the life you always have . . . regardless if you want to change or not. Most of us will just stay in our sleeping bags and then torture ourselves with regret for the rest of the day.

An example from my world finds me sitting in my chair too long in the early mornings, instead of getting out into the cold garage to work out—I am actually doing it right now . . . ugh. The headline my mind sends me is, "Just sit in the chair and read a little longer before you go workout. It's OK, finish the rest of your coffee." Thirty minutes later I am still in my chair and have now created a time crunch to get my workout in before my workday. I have learned how to override this headline most mornings (obviously not this morning . . . ugh), but it always takes the awareness that it's happening before I can overwrite the conditioned script of stay comfortable. When I become aware enough to override these scripts, I make decisions that better align with my goals and values—get in the gym on time and work out.

Our minds are creating everything we experience in our lives. It does this by taking the sensory input from our environment and turning that input into things like light, color, feel, heat, cold, and taste. It's amazing if you stop to think about it. A three-pound organ that is surrounded by bone and secluded in a dark space with no access to the outside world can receive vibrations from the surrounding environment and turn those vibrations into the elaborate experience we are having at this very moment. You are experiencing these words because your brain is processing the data entering your visual sensory system, running that data through a few filters that you have been creating your entire life (the ability to read words and understand their meaning), and creating an experience that looks and feels just like . . . well . . . reality.

A similar process is happening in the brain for each of our other senses as well. It stitches together all our sensory input, but it also includes many other pieces of unconscious data as it's computing, integrating, clipping, cropping, and finally creating the experience we call reality. My GoPro camera does something similar when I am filming with the stabilization turned on high. It records what I point it at, but it crops off a certain percentage of the outside frame to give the appearance of stability. In reality, it just removed what it wanted and left what it needed to complete the scene. Our brains act in much the same manner, but the secret is, it does all of it without our conscious input. Just like you don't consciously control your heartbeat or digestion, the brain is running on autopilot and we are only experiencing the headlines from the millions of processes being computed in our brains each day.

This is why humans are so amazing. We can focus our attention when required, but most thoughts and decisions are computed outside of our awareness. Otherwise, we would become overwhelmed with simple things like having to control how our hands are moving when brushing our teeth, or how much pressure to apply to the gas pedal to keep us steady at 45 miles per hour.

The other item worth noting is that all these unconscious processes make the brain the largest user of energy of any other organ in the body. It's estimated that the brain uses upwards of 20 to 25 percent of our total energy expenditure during a normal day.[2] An organ that equals only two percent of our body weight consumes a quarter of our energy. Remember this statistic as the book progresses. It will become important as we talk about times when our energy is waning and leaving us at the mercy of our emotions.

With all of that said, instead of diving deep into the brain and looking at all the subcomponents that control the conscious and unconscious mind, we are going to use a simple metaphor that I predict will be useful for everyone reading this book. With this metaphor, we can gain an understanding of what is happening behind the scenes in our minds and use this understanding to flourish during our long-distance experience. It will be so simple and intuitive that you will learn to dissect the moments when one part of your mind is running out of control. If we can catch these instances before the script runs too long, we can prevent much of the mental suffering on our journey. We can fill our days with more stillness and fulfillment rather than anxiety and anguish.

What is this metaphor? None other than the rider and the elephant. This metaphor submits that the rider is the rational part of our brain that can solve problems and plan the path forward. The elephant represents our emotional side and signifies the dominant role it plays in driving our behavior. The size difference between these two entities is strategic and illuminates the challenges we face in controlling our thoughts and behaviors.

The rider and the elephant metaphor is not new, and I am unfortunately not the genius who thought of it. It was created in the mind of psychologist Jonathan Haidt and made its entry into the world in his wonderful book, *The Happiness Hypothesis*. I think it's important to include Jonathan's explanation of this metaphor and how it came to be:

> The older metaphors about controlling animals work beautifully. The image that I came up with for myself, as I marveled at my weakness, was that I was a rider on the back of an elephant. I'm holding the reins in my hands, and by pulling one way or the other I can tell the elephant to turn, to stop, or to go. I can direct things, but only when the elephant doesn't have desires of his own. When the elephant really wants to do something, I'm no match for him.[3]

We can feel the power of this metaphor by his description of the small rational rider sitting atop this massive emotional beast. As he holds the reins, he can pull in the desired direction when he determines a change in path is necessary. However, if the giant elephant doesn't see the value in the change of direction, no amount of pulling, tugging, stressing, or pleading will get the six-ton animal to alter its course. This is the "it's cold in my tent and I ignore my alarm and stay inside my sleeping bag" example. If the two disagree on the way forward, the rider will lose every time unless he employs the right tools to coax the elephant down the desired path.

Hopefully, as you are in the initial stages of digesting this metaphor, you can predict its usefulness (by the way, that is your rider doing the predicting). We are going to spend the next few chapters explaining the rider and the elephant in more detail. We will also add one more component that I think will prove beneficial as well—the path.

I read about the addition of the path in the book, *Switch,* by co-authors and brothers Chip and Dan Heath. In their book, they teach people how to make significant changes by using the rider and the elephant metaphor, but they also added the path as a third component to the model. They posit that we can adjust the path in front of the rider and the elephant to help make a change easier, and as you will see later in this book, we can also use the path to help us reach our goals when needed. But first, let's look at how one famous researcher identifies the division (AKA the rider and elephant) we experience in our minds.

The Two Parts of Our Divided Minds

The first concept we need to accept before moving any further is that our minds are divided into two parts—the rational and the emotional mind. I first learned about this theory in Daniel Kahneman's book, *Thinking Fast and Slow.* He posited that the mind has two systems that are guiding our behavior: System 1 is the immediate, instinctive, and emotional part of our mind (the elephant). System 2 is the slower, rational, and deliberate part of our minds (the rider). For most of our daily thoughts and behaviors, System 1 is in the driver's seat. It's running off pre-programmed scripts that are either baked-in programs that we were born with (think fear responses) or habituated skills that require no conscious thought to perform (walking, brushing our teeth, etc.). The beauty of System 1 is that it doesn't require much energy to pull those scripts from their holding spots in the brain.

System 2 only kicks in when something has arisen that System 1 cannot handle, or when something unfamiliar comes into awareness that System 1 has little experience with. The key lesson

Kahneman's theory offered was that System 2 is often lazy and likes to conserve its limited energy. Therefore, if System 1 experiences a stimulus and develops an answer that feels suitable, System 2 will stay dormant and conserve energy.

An example Kahneman uses to show this is in the following problem:

> A bat and ball together cost $1.10. The bat costs one dollar more than the ball. How much does the ball cost?

Easy, right? Well, not really. If you quickly came up with 10 cents, then your System 2 was just fooled by System 1. The answer seemed so intuitive that your rational mind stayed dormant since your System 1 had it figured out. But in reality, it got it wrong. The answer is 5 cents. The bat has to cost one dollar more than the ball, therefore the bat costs $1.05 and the ball costs the remaining 5 cents (don't worry, only 50 percent of Harvard students get this problem right). Had your System 1 not been so sure it had the answer and had the answer not seemed so comfortable inside your mind, this dissonance would have nudged your System 2 for help.

Here is an example of that dissonance in problem form:

> What is 14 X 34?

Did you feel the cognitive friction kick in when you couldn't find the quick answer? This was because System 1 did a quick scan of its stored memories, knowledge, and experiences, and couldn't find a quick solution. Therefore, System 2 had to wake up and help figure out that the answer is 456. If you solved the problem by hand, both systems had to work in unison to solve the equation. System 1 was providing some rote multiplication solutions while System 2 was computing the more abstract pieces of the problem. However, if your System 2 is as lazy as mine, it figured if I just kept reading, the author would provide the answer for me—and I was right. Ahh, but once again, without using our System 2 when needed, we get lulled into a false reality as the answer is actually 476 . . . or is it?

Kahneman's theory reveals that our minds are running dual systems to help us manage our daily lives. Systems that will support and conflict with each other depending on many variables. One system runs autonomously and helps us carry out 99% of our daily required functions without expending a ton of energy, while the other system is primed and waiting to solve problems but can be extremely lazy and defers to the autonomous system more often than not. It's also a high consumer of energy when it turns on and conducts its problem-solving tasks.

For our application in the hiking context, I think Haidt's rider and elephant metaphor, with the addition of the Heath brothers' path component, pulls the goodness from Kahneman's theories and packages the info into a more digestible format for our purpose. However, I would also suggest reading the book, *Thinking Fast and Slow,* by Kahneman at some point. His research is fascinating and reveals many more realizations about our decisions and behaviors that we won't discuss in this book.

As we move forward, let me also put forth the idea that it's our two-part mind that often leaves us feeling disconnected from ourselves for much of our lives. The good news is that our bodies are always rooted in the present moment. We can't physically be anywhere else but right here, right now.

I am reminded of this every day as I stare out the window in front of my desk and see countless ducks carrying out their lives. They aren't believed to have the same "rider" functionality as humans, therefore, their biology keeps them tethered to their current place in the universe—tending to the needs of the moment. They aren't bogged down with regrets from the past, anxiety about what may happen in the future, or how their body looks today. They are running ancient software (as is our elephant) that keeps them focused on the basics of life—eat, drink, sleep, mate, and survive.

We are running this same software in the lower parts of our brain as well. It's what drives our elephant. But our rational mind (rider) keeps projecting our focus onto things other than the present moment. It constantly seeks to understand the present moment by comparing it to our memories. It seeks to predict the future by combining past experiences with current experiences. It's in these continuously running algorithms and scripts that we lose connection with our body in the present moment.

What if we could see how disconnected everyone's mind is from their body? Imagine if our heads remove themselves from our bodies and move toward our thoughts. Some of our heads would be behind our bodies because they are consumed with thoughts of the past. Others would be out in front of our bodies because they are anxious about the future. Very few bodies would actually have heads attached. Why? Because we are all consumed with thoughts from the past or future and are rarely in sync with our bodies. We leave our bodies to manage themselves while our minds are off time traveling and worrying about things that don't exist.

Why is this important to realize? Because as our rational, problem-solving mind projects itself into the past or future, the stories it creates trigger our nervous system as if those stories were actually true and happening in real-time. Let me say that another way. When we make up stories in our heads, our bodies often react as if the stories are true. If you ever laid awake at night because you felt stressed over a future project, or embarrassed over a perceived poor performance the day prior, then you have experienced what I am talking about here. Your body is in the present moment, lying in bed, tired and ready to sleep, but your mind is creating fake worlds and realities in your head.

These fake realities don't feel fake to the body because our nervous system reacts similarly to the way it reacts to real experiences. Your nervous system releases chemicals into your bloodstream as if the projections in your mind were happening. Your ancient mind just wants to sleep; your rational mind finds problems to solve and convinces your body to react accordingly. Thus, you lie awake while your body pumps cortisol and adrenaline through your system. It triggers your fear response and your body prepares for fight or flight. This is why understanding the two-part mind is so important.

It's no different on trail. Your mind will do battle with itself and your body will pay the price. However, there is hope if we can gain some awareness of these battles and determine ways to control the variables we have agency over. Let's look closer at the rider, elephant, and path components so we can gain a deeper understanding of their idiosyncrasies and start aiming their value towards our hiking experience.

A Quick Note

As we begin defining our rider and elephant, it's important to realize that I am grossly oversimplifying the brain for this discussion. I'm not trying to posit that our brains operate in these neat little silos and have no cross-functionality over these boundaries. They are far more complicated and interwoven, so stay at the surface with me and don't get wrapped around the axle if you are knowledgeable about the intricacies of brain functionality. Remember, the rider and the elephant are meant to be easy tools everyone can apply quickly and efficiently to battle mental chaos. If you want to learn more about the brain, look at my notes page at the end of the book for some good references.

Chapter Three
The Rider

For every complex problem, there is an answer that is clear, simple, and wrong.

H.L. Mencken

The Foundation

As the human animal evolved through history, only one part of the brain existed during all phases—what we now call the lower brain. You may have heard it called other names throughout the years like the reptilian, monkey, or primal brain. Our lower brain is focused on one thing and one thing only . . . survival. As the human evolved over millions of years, the lower brain kept taking in data and adjusting itself ever so slowly to increase our chances of survival. It gave us the ability to learn from and adjust to our environment so we had a better chance to reproduce and keep our species alive. Evolution, as Darwin discovered, is the manifestation of the work our lower brain has been accomplishing over the last few hundred thousand years.

It's important to note that the lower brain can't see into the future or predict consequences from actions. This is why evolution seems so painfully slow on the surface. It's a system that acts on instinct and nudges us toward behaviors that feel good in the present moment. In a modern context, this looks like our hand reaching for that doughnut or our car pulling into the drive-thru at McDonald's. We refer to this as bottom-up processing, meaning many of our thoughts and actions derive from the automatic lower brain. These are unconscious thoughts that happen outside of our awareness. It's the reason you can hike along a trail, keep your heart pumping blood, keep your lungs exchanging oxygen and carbon dioxide at the proper rate, digest your food, convert said food into energy, and regulate your body temperature . . . all without having to control any of it. Our autonomous nervous system does it all for us.

Thankfully, at some point in the recent past, when compared to the timeline of human existence, we began developing an outer layer to our brain known as the cortex. This top layer would give us more control over making logical decisions, suppressing the desires of our lower brain, predicting future outcomes by comparing past and present experiences, learning new information and integrating it in novel ways, and much, much more. If you have ever heard someone use the term "top-down processing," this is what they are referring to.

Top-down processing is the ability of our upper brain to recognize what the lower brain is up to and adjust its behaviors if it thinks there is a better path to take. It's the reasoning voice in our heads that suppresses the urge for the doughnut and aims our car away from McDonald's and towards healthier options. The upper brain is often our only hope to suppress some of the bad habits we have built in our lives. For me, my penchant for desserts is deeply entrenched in my lower brain. This means it's an emotion-driven behavior that takes a lot of energy to suppress. The only time I can override my hand reaching for dessert after dinner is to engage my more rational upper brain and use its strengths to keep me from shoving a cookie into my face.

But before we get too excited about this rationalization upgrade nature provided, we must remain cognizant that it is an early version of the software. Especially when compared to the firmware our autonomous lower brain is running. It still has many bugs that create obstacles in our lives. To paraphrase a point Jonathan Haidt made in his book *The Happiness Hypothesis*, a simple computer program can beat most humans in a game of chess, but there is no computer or robot in existence that can walk down a trail in the woods and express genuine emotions in the proper context.[4] In other words, our upper brain has good intentions and tries to help us solve complex problems, but often lacks the ability to factor in human emotions into its solutions. All the hype around emotional intelligence is not just a fad, but a requisite if we want to make better behavioral decisions.

Another important consideration is how much energy the upper brain requires to operate—upwards of 25 percent of our total energy expenditure. This cost in energy exists because our upper brain is always operating under the friction of problem-solving. It has to pull information from all over the brain to make its computations, and this consumes tons of energy. In contrast, the lower brain is running on a smooth path of conditioned responses and established pathways. Therefore, it doesn't require much energy to run these hard-wired scripts. When our energy stores become depleted, the rationalizing brain loses its ability to problem-solve effectively and leaves us at the mercy of the autonomic predispositions of our lower brain. When this happens, we often make poor decisions that are not in congruence with our goals and values once our exhaustion level starts elevating. It's not that you are a bad person because you avoided the gym after work, you just fell victim to your lower brain's headlines of "seek comfort and avoid pain."

These last few paragraphs hopefully set a rudimentary foundation for what is coming next. We will now begin using our rider (rationalizing upper brain) and elephant (autonomous lower brain) metaphor which should relieve us of too much more "scientificky" language.

The Rider

Perched on top of the elephant sits the problem-solving rider. His principal purpose in life is trying to predict where the elephant needs to go and convincing it to go there. He is only an advisor and has a limited capacity to alter the behavior of the elephant. You can imagine the rider's challenge; he weighs around 180 pounds and is trying to control an animal that weighs over six tons. Common sense reveals he can't use brute strength to get the elephant on the intended path. Instead, the rider must lean on his strengths of analyzing situations, rational thinking, and problem-solving to coax the elephant to move towards his vision. These strengths are extremely valuable, but they cost the rider exorbitant amounts of energy throughout the day. Therefore, he must be very deliberate about when to pull on the reins with force and when to relax his grip and let the elephant do its own thing.

The rider is also responsible for setting expectations for their journey. He constantly updates his calculations by comparing where he is currently, where he's been, and where he's trying to go. Once complete, he then tries to predict the best path forward. His ability to think about the future helps establish goals and define the direction in which to travel. He is also the voice of reason when temptations present themselves. Restraining the elephant from always taking the easy road, stopping for breaks too often, sleeping in when he should be hiking, or not leaving town because he doesn't want to hike today, all fall on the shoulders of the rider. As you can imagine, his job can be exhausting, especially when the elephant gets grumpy and belligerent—which never happens on a thru-hike . . . yeah, right. I tend to ride the grumpy bus in the late afternoons on a thru-hike, but more on that later.

For all his strengths and reliability, the rider is also beset with some hardy weaknesses. His default mode is searching for problems, and this tendency carries a bias towards looking for negativity in his environment. Rarely does the rider focus on positive events or waste his limited energy on positive accomplishments. Instead, he is on high alert for "what's wrong now and how can I fix it." This is not necessarily the mental state we are hoping for when hiking. Maybe most important for a thru-hiker, our rider's energy levels are finite, and once he gets tired, he loses his ability to problem-solve effectively. It takes a lot of willpower to maintain control of the animal he is riding, and when his energy and willpower get drained, poor decisions, or no decisions, are inevitable.

The rider is also plagued with emotional aloofness as he searches for solutions to the problems confronting him. This often puts his solutions at odds with the six-ton elephant he is trying to coax. When the elephant doesn't want to listen, the rider becomes a helpless passenger. If you are having a bad day on trail and feel emotionally wrecked inside, your rider will have a hard time developing a solution that seems rational and soothes your emotional chaos. He just doesn't have that upgrade yet. This is why the elephant's solutions often feel like the better option. I argue many quit their journey because of this.

Another weakness of the rider is the tendency to over-think and over-analyze things. Many of us are plagued with this software glitch. It often leads to an inability to make a decision because multiple solutions look appropriate. This often creates obstacles in our path and exhausts the rider's energy levels much earlier in the day. Remember, with the absence of guidance, the elephant will control our behavior autonomously. It is already hard-baked inside of us. It looks like your Matrix life being transplanted out onto the trail . . . and nobody should want that. Therefore, it's important to keep our rider online and operating as efficiently as possible. Our success on trail will depend on it.

Let's pull an example from the sitcom "Seinfeld" that shows how our rider's problem-solving propensities can spin into a weakness if we don't learn how to exert some control over him. In our example, we find George Costanza (one of Jerry Seinfeld's close friends played by the fantastic actor Jason Alexander) seeking therapy for some events that are happening in his life. As his therapist invites him to sit down on the couch, he tries to unzip his coat to get a little more comfortable. The therapist asks George some standard questions, but George can't get his zipper undone—it was stuck on a piece of cloth next to his zipper. Here is the conversation as it played out. Notice what George's rider is doing inside his head and how his elephant gets triggered and jumps in.

> GEORGE: What's with this damn zipper?
>
> DANA (Therapist): (Saying calmly) It doesn't matter. You'll fix it later. Tell me about your girlfriend.
>
> GEORGE: (Getting more aggravated) It's stuck on a piece of cloth. I can't get the cloth out.
>
> DANA: (Still calm) It doesn't matter, so…
>
> GEORGE: (Thrashing with his zipper) This is a brand-new jacket. Boy, this really burns me up!
>
> DANA: (Calmly but more direct) George, George . . . look at me. OK. Forget about the zipper. What's your girlfriend's name? (She redirected George's rider)
>
> GEORGE: (Settling down, realizing what was happening and smiling, and then focusing on Dana and her question) Susan.
>
> DANA: (Satisfied and laughing with George) OK,

> We're getting somewhere.
>
> GEORGE: (Ramps right back up grabbing at his zipper) It's just SO frustrating! It's a brand-new jacket!

Haha, I'm laughing just thinking about how consumed his rider became with solving the zipper problem and how his elephant's emotions jumped feet first into the drama. Dana was using her rider to reason with George and bring his focus to the actual problem he came to solve, but she wasn't getting through. His rider wasn't having any of it until it fixed the problem at hand, and it also triggered the emotional elephant to assist in the effort of freeing his zipper. Such a classic example of what happens when we lose cognitive control and let our rider's penchant for problem-solving run wild.

So, what happened next in the therapy session? One would think Dana would continue to use her rider to convince George to let the zipper fade from his focus. After all, she is the professional in the room. However, by the time the scene transitioned to the other storyline in the show, and then back to George and Dana, we now find Dana standing over George on the couch frantically wrestling with his zipper . . . and wrestling with her rider and elephant as well.

> DANA: (Growing frustrated) You see, it's got a little piece of cloth stuck underneath. (Begins pulling harder on the zipper)
>
> GEORGE: (Somewhat calmly) Can you just pull it up a little?
>
> DANA: Ugh . . . here, no wait, you hold it (pulls harder), hold it (pulls even harder), Dammit! I can't move it (grimacing from the exertion), I have never seen a zipper so stubborn! (pulls more

aggressively) Dammit! I almost had it!

GEORGE: (His rider updated its focus on a new problem—his new coat might rip) No, no, that will make it separate . . . you're going to rip it . . . you're going to rip it!

DANA: (Gives one last attempt in a full frenzy) UGH!!! (Standing over George, she takes a deep breath and calms down) I think we are going to have to stop.

GEORGE: (In a very feeble tone) OK.

What we see play out so eloquently in the zipper fiasco is how our rider instinctively finds problems to solve and we often have a hard time focusing on anything else. So much so that those around us adopt our problems as if they were their own. This is because the frustration of the zipper not only brought out the worst in George's rider, but it got the emotional elephant involved as well. And once the elephant joined in, it was all over. But why did we see Dana get sucked into the zipper problem in the next scene when she seemed like her rider was firmly in control?

Our rider loves solving problems, and our emotions are contagious. If the rider can't find his own problem to solve, he will help someone else try to solve theirs. This sounds like a good thing for hikers when hiking a long-distance trail. If I am having a tough time figuring out a solution, maybe a fellow hiker can employ their rider and help me figure it out. However, any long-distance hiker can recount times when a certain hiker on trail always seemed to have a problem and needed help.

I witnessed this at a few shelters and hostels early in my hike on the AT. (I theorize it only happened early on the trail because those with the "always had a problem" trait rarely made it too far into their thru-hike.) This can become a repellent and you will often see these "problem-consumed" hikers become isolated because word on the trail spreads fast. This begs the question: how can we avoid being consumed by our rider's tendencies? How can we avoid getting sucked into the negatives of the problems surrounding us?

The good news is, there are ways to gain some control over our rider and keep him moving forward towards our goals. In their book *Switch*, Dan and Chip Heath provide three methods to help direct our rider to be more effective in his duties.

The first tip is to nudge the rider to find the bright spots and follow them. By this they mean if we can identify what is already working, then we should do more of that and not focus on all the negative problems that seem to keep popping up. For example, if I'm a week into my thru-hike and I still can't reach my goal of averaging 10 miles a day, I should focus on the things that have proven helpful versus focusing on things I can't control. Therefore, if I noticed I was able to hike more miles when I started hiking an hour earlier than normal, then I should do more of that instead of getting trapped in the "everybody is better than me and I'm never going to make it" funnel of negative thinking. These solutions seem obvious when we are reading these pages in our warm comfortable chairs, but tons of hikers drop off trail because their riders became absorbed in all the negatives and couldn't see the bright spots. Find what's working and do more of it.

The second method the Heath brothers suggest is to script the critical moves. Think about this as establishing small behavioral contracts with yourself that will be easy for the elephant to accept and won't zap the energy of your rider. Decisions like filtering tomorrow morning's water before climbing in your tent at night, establishing a soft (meaning firm but flexible) hiking plan for the next day, going to bed by 8:00 p.m. so you can get up early and hike longer, and hitting the release valve on your sleeping pad as soon as your alarm goes off. All these little contracts save your rider the energy he will need to make bigger decisions later in the day. Remember, every decision costs the rider some of his finite energy, and by scripting some of the easier choices, we can reserve energy for later. Some people think time, water, and food are the most valuable commodities on a thru-hike. I suggest that energy is our most critical resource. It drives every action and decision we make at a biological level.

The third tip reveals our rider has to use all the tools at his disposal in setting the direction and nudging the elephant to the correct path. To do this, the rider must lean on more than just his rational decisions that are often lacking the emotional appeal the elephant requires. It's the rider's ability to conduct analysis, set direction, and appeal to the emotional elephant that achieves unity and success.

For all those reading this and thinking, "I don't have time to sit there and play emotional touchy-feely when it's time to solve problems," just remember that 75 percent of people drop off trail (most within 300 miles of their start point) because they couldn't adapt to the demands of the experience. Whether we like it or not, we are emotional creatures, and the elephant controls the systems that guide most of our behavior. To think you can problem-solve your way up the trail without catering to the needs of your elephant is simply ignoring the reality of the situation. Those who learn to direct the rider and coax the elephant are the ones who have the best shot at making it to Katahdin, kissing the sign, and raising their hands in victory.

Don't worry. If you aren't the type of person who is adept at tending to the emotional side of human nature, we will discuss some helpful tips as the book progresses. Personally, I lean on the alter ego effect in those moments (Chapter 14).

Now that we have a better understanding of the strengths and weaknesses of our rider, let's shift toward the elephant and learn how it controls the lion's share of our behavior . . . and arguably, our life.

Chapter Four
The Elephant

The world is ruled, and the destiny of civilization is established, by the human emotions.

Napoleon Hill

The elephant weighs approximately six tons and is a powerful, tireless, and difficult animal to direct. It represents the primal part of us that drives much of our behavior.[5] It's the System 1 part of our mind that reacts instantly to the environment and has little control over its conditioned responses. If you've ever jumped back in fear when you see a long, thin, squiggly object on the ground in front of you, this was your elephant trying to save you. We have no control over this reaction . . . it's hard-baked inside our ancient brain. It's much faster than our System 2 rider, who is still trying to figure out if it was a root or a snake stretching across the trail. These differences in response times make managing our minds even more difficult.

The elephant is emotional, irrational, and very stubborn. This requires the rider to spend excessive amounts of energy to convince the elephant to alter its course. The elephant likes normalcy and comfort, therefore, when we try to disrupt his inertia, the elephant resists and refuses to move. He can't see into the future and will stay fixated on carrying out its normal safety and survival routines if the rider doesn't include sound reasoning, worthy guidance, and emotional subtlety in his commands.

This is why building appropriate rituals and habits are vital in overcoming the elephant's inertia. Without them, the elephant will remain dominant over the rider and our forward progress will be stunted. Habit expert James Clear found that the average time it takes a human to instill a new habit is approximately 66 days.[6] This is the average time it takes to push a new behavior down into the subconscious level where the elephant accepts it without resistance. This obviously varies with the habit you are trying to create, but 66 days is a good estimate to use for our discussion.

Example: If getting up earlier is the behavior you want to change on trail, you will need to script the critical moves (ahh, directing the rider) of how you will influence yourself to wake up at the desired time. This could be a simple ritual of placing your phone at the other end of your tent so you have to sit up to turn off the alarm. You could have all your clothes laid out and ready to put on. You could prime your stove and water so you can fire up some caffeine as soon as your eyes open. The more you have to think about individual behaviors, the bigger vote the elephant gets in completing those actions. If it's something he doesn't want to do in the moment, he will override any decision your rider is trying to make.

For me, when it's time to wake up on trail, I simply reach up and open the valve on my sleeping pad and listen to it deflate. This became a reflexive habit by the time I made it to the town of Hot Springs, North Carolina, which is around the 275-mile mark on the AT. Most of us can't sleep when lying on the cold, hard ground. Any hiker that uses this "critical move" to force themselves awake can attest to how disheartening it is to hear the air escaping from their pad. There are tons of little rituals you can establish to overcome the inertia of your giant elephant. We will discuss more habits and rituals throughout the book.

Hopefully, you are gaining some comprehension of how stubborn our elephants can be. It takes weeks to change a habit or instill a new one. Why? Because our elephant expects normalcy and likes to feel comfortable and safe. But we usually don't start these journeys intending to be comfortable and safe. We start them to incite adventure, change, and growth. However, growth can't happen when we are being guided by the elephant's agenda. Growth only happens when we push ourselves into spaces that are uncomfortable and risky. Growth takes time, and time is the one variable that most aspiring thru-hikers struggle with the most.

If we overlay James Clear's habit theory on top of the thru-hiking context, it makes total sense. How many hikers decide to quit before their 66th day on trail? A remarkably high percentage. How many drop out after the 66-day mark? Very few. Obviously, the number of days it takes to get adapted to our new hiking identity is different for each of us, but the point is still valid. Controlling the elephant is difficult, but it serves as a critical component to our success on trail . . . and in life. If we can discover ways to adapt to trail life more readily, we stand a much better chance of reaching that far terminus, or whatever goals we seek.

If our elephant continues to act on the same automatic processes from our Matrix life—comfort-seeking, pain avoidance, and always searching for the path of least resistance—then our chances of finding success reduce significantly. Our rider can point to the change of identity we want to make, but it's the elephant that must transform into a long-distance hiker.

Like the rider, the elephant brings some positive qualities to our journey as well. He's our source of beautiful emotions like love, gratitude, empathy, and loyalty, all of which enrich our lives and the lives of those around us. For this book, we will focus on how to aim these positive emotions inward to help soothe the mental damage created by the overcritical rider. I argue, it's only when we can aim the elephant's love, compassion, and sympathy towards ourselves that we can overcome those days we aren't able to accomplish all the goals our rider predicted for us. Self-compassion—the ability to extend compassion to oneself in instances of perceived inadequacy, failure, or general suffering—is a trait many of us lack in our daily lives.

I had little self-compassion for myself when I started my thru-hike on the AT. That shouldn't surprise anyone because when you grow up in the special operations sector of the military, self-compassion is often perceived as a manifestation of weakness, not strength. However, I quickly learned how important self-compassion would be when trying to complete such a grueling and lengthy journey like a thru-hike.

If you attempt a challenge of this magnitude without the ability to be self-compassionate during your times of struggle, you will suffer immeasurably and erode your ability to keep pushing forward. Your focus will narrow to all the things you don't have instead of all the things you do have. This is where we fall into the fatal funnel of despair, and once inside, most hikers are doomed. However, if we can become habituated to employ our elephant's powerful tools towards the rider's penchant for negativity, then we can use things like self-compassion as a balm for the mental cuts the rider unwittingly inflicts upon us.

Our elephant controls this self-healing ability. But we can only tap into the strength of our elephant if we are aware enough to realize we need it. Our emotions are the foundational power that pushes us towards our goals on these grueling journeys. The elephant is such an enormous piece of our roadmap to success, but if we don't train our rider in the art of properly advising this magnificent beast, it will run amok and cause chaos in our lives. Let's look at a situation that shows how damaging it can be when the rider loses control over the elephant.

The Western States 100 Endurance Race

My wife and I like to watch ultramarathons on YouTube for entertainment. For those who are unfamiliar with these races, an ultramarathon (ultra for short) is any race longer than the regular marathon distance of 26.2 miles. In particular, we like to watch 100-mile endurance races in mountainous terrain. These races seem to test the runners' mental strength in a similar way to a long-distance thru-hike but compressed into a 24 to 36-hour timeframe.

I think it's odd that I enjoy watching these races so much because I have always detested running. This dislike was incited in the early days of my induction into Marine Reconnaissance, where we ran an average of 8-10 miles a day—every single freaking day. But what draws me into the world of endurance racing is the mental side of these extreme challenges.

To be honest, it's the mental side that draws me into hiking long-distance trails as well. It's an excuse to avoid running but still challenge the mind in ways inconceivable to most humans. It's why I choose to hike 20 to 25 miles a day during my hikes. It's during these extreme challenges that we can experience the real inner chaos being waged between the rider and the elephant. If we can gain an awareness of the chaos as it starts, we can employ techniques to optimize the relationship between the rider and the elephant. When we can apply the right tools at the right time, our mental suffering decreases, our forward momentum increases, and our joy, fulfillment, and stillness can establish a strong foothold in our mental space.

An example of the elephant's power to overtake the rider's logical strategy showed up in a Western States 100 video we watched a few nights ago. As runners make their way over this 100-mile course, they encounter multiple support stations positioned along their path. These stations allow the runners to resupply, eat, change socks and shoes, and ready themselves for the next difficult leg of the race. The hydration and nutrition plan between these checkpoints is essential in ensuring the runners can perform at optimal levels throughout the course. If they don't grab enough food, drink, or supplements for the next leg, they take the chance of bonking before the next support stop.

In the thru-hiking context, it's comparable to hikers having to stop in towns to resupply and making sure they outfit themselves properly for the next multi-day leg of the trail. Get it wrong, and you will be blessed with a surfeit of mental suffering caused by poor decisions. When the rider or elephant guide us to poor decisions, mental suffering is a forgone conclusion.

The runners in these ultra races use support teams that meet them at the checkpoints that allow crew access. Here, they help the athletes refit and resupply for the next leg of the race. They will then leapfrog to the next checkpoint to await their runner's arrival and do it all over again. Along with these personal support teams, the race has a group of core volunteers that provide general support to all runners. Here is the list of the hydration and nutrition support these aid stations provide to all runners. This information is from the Western States 100 website:

> The aid stations are well stocked with fluids and a variety of foods. The generally available fluids are water, Clif Shot Hydration Drink, Clif Shot Recovery Drink, Sprite or 7Up, and Coke. The night aid stations will also have soup, hot coffee, and hot chocolate. The foods that are generally available are: salt replacement foods (saltines, pretzels, chips), Clif Bars, Clif Mojo Bars, Clif Shot Energy Gels, Clif Shot Bloks, fruits

(oranges, bananas, melons), potatoes, cookies, candies, sandwiches, etc.

If your support crew doesn't make it to the next checkpoint, or you are at a checkpoint without crew access, there are still tons of supplies available to each runner. That's if the runner's elephant doesn't get emotionally triggered when their crew is a no-show at a pre-planned checkpoint.

As the video progressed, we got to watch the runners making it to checkpoint Duncan Canyon at mile 24. This was a fun checkpoint to watch because it was still early in the day and the race leaders are still smiling and seem in good mental shape—even though they had already put 24 miles behind them. As we watched the runners cycling through their pit stops, the female in second place arrived at Duncan Canyon and was frantically looking for her crew. The camera stayed on her as some race supporters approached to ask what she needed. All she kept saying was, "I need my crew." Once she realized her crew hadn't made it to the checkpoint for support, she proceeded down the trail with only one small flask of water and a couple of gels from a nearby support tent. She clearly did not have what she needed for the next tough leg of the race, but she left the Duncan Canyon checkpoint anyway.

As any good thru-hiker would do when watching this, I compared her actions to a thru-hiker that is running low on supplies and blows past a town stop when the next town is days away. It makes no sense, but when the elephant gets triggered, its actions and decisions are often irrational and downright dangerous. Remember, the elephant can't see into the future and his actions are focused on measuring the present through a filter of the past. As we could see playing out on the video, her missing crew support triggered her elephant significantly. Being an elite ultrarunner, her rider knew she shouldn't leave without pausing and developing an impromptu hydration and nutrition plan for the next leg, but it seems her triggered elephant took over all mental processing.

To no surprise, she had a rough leg into the next checkpoint. She was dehydrated and mentally beaten down upon arrival. To make matters worse, her elephant was still in control of her mental space. Instead of focusing on prepping for what's next, she was stuck in the past. She kept verbally ruminating about how her crew wasn't at the last checkpoint and she had been out of water and nutrition for 45 minutes. Her elephant was clinging to the emotional pain of her last checkpoint experience and overriding her rider's ability to problem-solve for the future.

Thankfully, some of her friends and crew members were trying to nudge her rider back into the cockpit by reassuring her she was OK and could still get back in the race. This was a perfect response from her crew because they were trying to arrest her descent inside the fatal funnel that her elephant was dragging her into. However, she continued pushing back against their nudges and kept trying to make them see how damaging it was that her crew wasn't at the prior checkpoint. Her elephant wanted others to feel the pain she was experiencing in the moment. The problem with this was that she was falling farther behind the race leader and seemed to have a "victim" script looping inside her mind. She needed her rider to take back control.

How could she have prevented the rider from getting overtaken by the elephant when a contingency happened during the race? I suggest she could have done two things that could have prevented her elephant from becoming triggered: 1) she could have let go of the expectation that her crew would always be there; 2) she could have scripted the critical moves for the rider. As we will discuss in more detail later in the book, our expectations are trigger mechanisms for our elephant. If she had prepped herself mentally that her crew was not a 100 percent guarantee, then her elephant wouldn't have felt so betrayed. To prepare for the absent crew contingency, she could have had a pre-planned checklist of what to grab from the race support stations in case her support team couldn't make it to the checkpoint. When our expectations aren't met, or we don't give the rider a script, we leave ourselves at the mercy of the elephant, who, when triggered, can turn our lives sideways in an instant. At mile 24 of this incredibly hard race, she unconsciously unleashed her elephant and would spend much of the remaining miles trying to get her negative emotions contained and her elephant back on the correct path.

The questions this scenario presents are: How will you handle your elephant when it goes out of control on trail? Do you know what your emotional triggers are before you begin your hike? What are the things in your Matrix life that seem to suppress your rider and trigger your elephant?

For me, when my plan doesn't come to fruition, I tend to get anxious and upset. I look for things to blame and I will push myself, often to extreme levels, to get things back on track. For example, if I woke up on trail and planned on hiking 25 miles that day, I would get triggered if I didn't make that goal. The problem, you can imagine, is that the later in the day it became, the less energy my rider had to make rational decisions. This usually meant that as I grew tired, the realization that I wouldn't make my distance goal triggered my elephant and would wreak havoc in my mind. How did I learn to overcome this? I scripted the critical moves to help get my rider back in the pilot seat. Once back in control, the rider could help keep my emotional elephant tamed.

The script I used in this scenario would find me checking my phone for LTE reception while I was still hiking. When I found enough reception to make a call, I would stop and take a break. I would pull out a high-calorie snack, pour some electrolyte mix in my water bottle, and call my wife. This script helped get some needed nutrition and hydration into my body, which reduced some of the friction in my mind. The phone call home would help level my mental bubbles because my wife always knew how to talk me off the emotional ledge. Her soothing voice would rob the energy from my elephant and help my rider climb back into the pilot seat.

The phrase she would always say is, "Everything at home is fine. Taking one more day out there won't hurt us back here. Just focus on you and know that we support you 100%."

You can hopefully picture how those words can soothe the anxiety I would feel when I was not meeting my distance goals on trail. As a married man with a family at home, I was emotionally invested in getting back home to "help" them as fast as possible. This would create a giant trigger button for my elephant and would test me to my core during many days on trail. Scripting my critical moves when the wave of emotions hit saved my hike.

What if I couldn't find cell coverage during those moments? Good question. My script for eating and drinking electrolytes stayed the same. We often lose cognitive control on trail because we let our hydration and nutrition become unbalanced throughout the day. It happens so slowly that it creeps up on us and, before we know it, our rider is offline and our elephant is triggered. Therefore, if you notice mental friction increasing during your hiking day, create a ritual of forcing food and electrolytes into your system to help reduce the effects. At best, it can help get your rider back online. At worst, you are still getting hydrated and providing yourself with energy for the miles you have left for the day. There is no downside to this ritual.

If cell service wasn't available and I couldn't call my wife, I would break out my AT guidebook and start reassessing my reality. I noticed that when I am hiking, my mind would start creating a negative story of how far behind I am getting and how I'm failing to meet my rider's expectations. But once I saw the trail laid out linearly in my guidebook, it always arrested my descent into the funnel. I could see the plethora of options that existed, and it helped calm my emotional elephant. With my elephant calmed down, my rider could come back online and have a rational look at what was possible for the rest of the day.

As I matured as a hiker on my journey northbound, I learned how important it was to keep the elephant's negative emotions in check. I also learned how to lean on my elephant's strengths to help reduce my mental friction and remove the self-generated obstacles from my path. The rider and the elephant must work in unison if we have any hope of walking 2,200 miles over many months.

We must also remember that the elephant is a "feeling" entity, and the only way to get it on board is to cater to its emotional needs. We know the rider needs direction, but directions don't work on the elephant . . . it needs motivation. Not the "You can do it!" rah-rah speeches that we often think about, but motivation from accomplishing small goals and feeling the emotions that accompany these victories. The elephant isn't concerned with checking off items on a mental checklist. It needs to FEEL the goodness that comes with accomplishing the little steps along the path. You won't talk the elephant out of quitting something when it's hell-bent on quitting. Our elephants don't give a rat's ass about the adage "Don't quit on a bad day."

That's why most of the hiking tips you read in books and online aren't able to keep 75 percent of the hikers on trail when things get hard. It's not because the advice is bad or doesn't work, it's because the hikers try to apply it without understanding the two parts of their mind and how to manage the rider and the elephant when needed. The saying, "Don't quit on a bad day," will often fail unless we understand this phrase is aimed directly at the rational system (rider) in our mind. But in those low moments, when it feels like everything is collapsing down on top of us, our rider is usually offline and of little help to our situation.

It's the elephant we should appeal to in these moments, and he wants instant gratification. To the elephant, there is no waiting until tomorrow . . . it's miserable and wants to quit NOW! Suppressing this urge to quit is the rider's business, and if he is offline or busy, good luck at preventing your elephant from quitting.

Understanding this is the first step to preventing what comes next—quitting on a bad day. We will discuss more tips on appealing to the elephant as the book progresses. Stay patient, understanding the foundation of your mind **IS** the secret to overcoming its weaknesses on your hike.

Now that we have a foundational grasp on the rider and the elephant, let's shift focus to the third component in our metaphor and learn how to set the conditions on the path in front of us. The AT, or any other long-duration event, are hard enough without the inadvertent mental obstacles that we inject into the experience. By understanding how to create conditions for success in front of us, we can reduce the friction for the rider and the elephant and increase our forward momentum.

Chapter Five
The Path

The great way is not difficult for those who have no preferences. Make the slightest distinction, however, and heaven and Earth are set infinitely apart.

Hsin Hsin Ming

The path in our metaphor does not refer to a tangible path like the AT or other trails. It relates more to creating the prime environment for both the rider and elephant to move towards an agreed upon goal with as little resistance as possible. This "goal" could be anything from reaching Katahdin, the Canadian border, or the end of a long military deployment. If we prime the environment effectively, we reduce the energy required to direct the rider or coax the elephant towards our goals. The trick, however, is that both the rider and the elephant must agree on a clear direction forward. When they disagree, mental chaos ensues and stunts our forward momentum. When this happens, getting our minds back on the desired path becomes much harder.

It's also important to note that every problem we encounter is not always a rider or an elephant problem. Sometimes, the destination is clear, and the elephant is on board, but things outside of our control create friction on our path. Therefore, understanding what's inside and outside our span of control is important on our journey. If our rider tries to solve a problem that he has no control over, or if our elephant gets emotional over a rainstorm or the terrain, then we waste precious energy resisting things we cannot change. This often finds us flailing about helplessly and making impulsive decisions that don't serve our goal.

As an example, imagine you set a goal of hiking 15 miles today to reach the next town. All you can think about is getting some town food, a hot shower, doing some laundry, and charging your electronics. Your rider sets the direction, your elephant is on board with thoughts of comfort and luxury, but the trail is exceedingly rocky and difficult. After a short time, it becomes obvious you are not making the progress you had hoped for. To make it into town at a decent hour, you decide to forgo all breaks and even skip lunch. As the day progresses, you hit some steep climbs that wreck you both mentally and physically. Then you notice dark clouds building above you and hear thunder getting closer and closer. You push harder and try to muster every ounce of energy towards getting to town as fast as possible. However, the mountains don't get any less steep and the thunderstorm unleashes its torrents of rain and wind upon you. With several miles left to reach the road into town, you feel dejected and exhausted. You aren't sure you can make it the rest of the way because of your deteriorating physical and mental shape. You start blaming the trail and weather for your miserable predicament. Clearly, this is not the mental space we want to find ourselves in.

Let's dissect this situation using our metaphor. The rider set the goal of 15 miles, which is usually very doable. The elephant wants the comfort of town, so getting him on board was easy. However, the environmental structure (steep climbs and thunderstorms) would throw some mental chaos into the mix. The question is, Did we make the appropriate decisions to keep our rider and elephant satiated while adjusting to the conditions outside of our control—the tough terrain and weather? The decision to push harder and skip lunch was a risky move that will affect our ability to rationalize and manage our emotions. Depleting the body of nutrition and hydration when hiking is a sure way to create obstacles in our path.

A tired and nutrient-deficient rider won't make rational decisions when required. Instead of making a rational decision to seek shelter from the weather, our decision to push harder and remain on trail during the storm simply added more chaos to the situation. When the only decision we leave ourselves is to hike faster and throw all caution to the wind, we have effectively shot ourselves in the foot. We can't control the trail conditions or the weather, however, we can control how we plan for and adjust to these obstacles. If we plan and adapt successfully, we can avoid creating the mental chaos that will manifest when we make irrational and reactive decisions.

So, how can we shape our path to ensure our rider and elephant can adapt faster, experience less friction, and find more fulfillment? First, we must tweak the environment to reduce the obstacles we face. It's important to remember that we can only tweak the things within our control. I can't change the terrain, rocks, ice, snow, heat, bugs, mud, and rain, but I can control how I react to them. I can strategize my day to lessen the negative effects on my mind and body. Second, we must build habits that help ease the friction on both the rider and elephant. Understanding how bad habits create friction, and how good habits eliminate friction, will prove critical in reaching our goals. With these two techniques in hand, let's return to the scenario and see how we can apply them.

It's clear from this scenario that we created unnecessary obstacles for ourselves as we tried to reach town. Had we been deliberate, we could have planned around the known obstacles that we don't control—the terrain and weather. We could have used our guidebook or Guthook app to get a sense of the terrain's difficulty. We could have also obtained a weather forecast if we had a cell signal. By understanding the terrain and weather, we can predict the obstacles our rider and elephant will face on our path into town.

I know I can't control the terrain or weather, but I do control how I react to them when they present themselves to me. Much like the ultrarunner who should have scripted the critical moves at the aid station in the previous chapter, if I understand the obstacles in my path, I can script the moves that will keep my rider and elephant in harmony when the chaos hits. Using a script helps me tweak the parts of the environment that I control.

My script in this situation would have been simple. I would wake up uber early and give myself more time to complete the 15 miles and still make it to town at a reasonable hour. The early start would also allow me to avoid the storms predicted for the afternoon. However, we often fail to see these simple solutions because our habits of sleeping in are too strong to overcome. Our elephant's desire for comfort usually overrides the rider's plea to solve the day's problems in a better way. That's why building good habits are so important in reducing the friction on the path in front of you. If we can't do something as simple as waking up earlier when it benefits us, then the options at our disposal are reduced significantly. It often places the elephant as the primary decision-maker because we are unconsciously drawn to our proclivity for comfort and ease. When we let our elephant be the decision-maker, we often find ourselves stuck in the ruts of our Matrix life. The same life many of us desired to change by entering the arena of a thru-hike.

When considering the threat of thunderstorms, I would have scripted the plan to stop, set up my tent, and wait out the storm while eating snacks and drinking coffee. Since I started my hiking day earlier, my elephant won't trigger as easily because it knows there is still time to make it to town to enjoy the comforts awaiting us. That's not to discount the challenges my elephant will present .

. . my elephant can be a big, whiny baby at times like this, but my script will help to assuage its anxiety in a measurable way.

As you can hopefully see, scripting the critical moves helps us tweak our environment and react more appropriately to the obstacles on our path. If we prime the decisions beforehand, we keep our elephant less emotional and save the rider's energy from being wasted on making decisions during the chaos. Therefore, all we have to do when confronted with these obstacles is execute the plan.

I encountered something like this when I reached New Hampshire's White Mountains (dubbed "The Whites") on my thru-hike. I arrived there early in the hiking season (I got there in the middle of May which is early by thru-hiking standards) and there was still tons of snow piled up on the trail when I arrived. I was anxious as I approached this section of trail because it's known in the hiking community as being exceptionally difficult. The Whites also experienced heavy snowfall amounts during the winter, so I kept questioning whether I should just bypass this section and hike it after I summit Katahdin. My rider convinced me to give it a shot but to always have an escape plan if conditions were too extreme. That sounds good in theory, but let's watch how it played out on trail.

As I climbed Mount Moosilauke—the official start of The Whites on a northbound hike of the AT—I encountered little patches of snow in the shady areas of the summit. So far, this was nothing I couldn't easily handle. After taking the requisite pictures of the expansive views on top, I started heading down the north side of the mountain, which is known for its ridiculous steepness. I argue, descending the north side of Moosilauke is the steepest descent on the entire trail (minus Katahdin). How steep is it you ask? According to the AT Guidebook, when a hiker hits the steepest part of the descent, they lose over 2,200 feet of elevation in less than a mile. To add some scientific descriptions to help validate how dramatic it is to lose 2,200 feet in less than a mile . . . that's hella STEEP!

To make matters worse, snow and ice still covered the trail, and it was treacherous beyond description. The path looked like a super narrow ski slope, but instead of fluffy snow that would have made achieving footholds a little easier, it was a sheet of compacted ice. Walking off to the side of the trail wasn't an option in most spots because the treeline and dense vegetation came right up to the edge of the path. The few parts of the trail that were not covered by snow were usually rocky areas that were wet and slippery. What I was left with, as I stared down this ridiculously steep and icy descent, was a difficult decision on how to handle the situation.

As mentioned earlier, I made a pact with myself that if I encountered winter conditions that threatened my safety and ability to complete this hike, I should think about bypassing this 80-mile section of trail and come back after I summit Katahdin. This is where scripting the critical moves can prevent our rider from having to make hard decisions when his energy and self-control are in a depleted state. To add a bit of context, this was my third hard hiking day in a row and my body and mind were getting exhausted. This put my rider at a tremendous disadvantage when I leaned on him to make a decision on Moosilauke.

But here's the key lesson for all of us: Thinking about something and scripting out the actual moves are NOT the same thing. Yes, I had been wise to consider bypassing arguably the most dangerous part of the AT when it still had snow and ice present, but I stopped short of scripting out the plan if and when I first encountered said snow and ice. I had the chance to tweak my environment and reduce the friction on my path but left the decision to my rider when he was depleted and unable to think clearly. This left the decision to the emotional elephant who could only think about moving in the direction that would get him to town the fastest—down the most dangerous mile of trail one could arguably encounter.

So, as I stood there with a critical decision staring me in the face, I knew that town was only one more day away, and the sooner I made it off that mountain, the quicker I could get in my tent, eat, recover, and wake the next day to make it to town by early evening. That's how it went down. My elephant took over the decision because my rider was exhausted. Therefore, we spent the next two hours descending the most treacherous piece of terrain I had ever navigated in my life.

There were two different occasions during my descent that I had fallen and began sliding so fast that I could not arrest myself until I careened into some trees. One of those two times, I was heading for a huge drop-off that would have sent me down a 20-foot cliff into the creek running beside the trail. I was able to grab a couple of trees to prevent that from happening but was less than 15 feet from the cliff when I finally stopped sliding. This is what can happen when we leave our decisions up to chance on our hikes. Had I scripted the critical moves before I encountered the situation, I would have simply turned around and descended another trail and attacked this section another day. But I didn't, and I am lucky as hell I didn't get seriously injured or even worse.

If you want to watch this day on my YouTube channel, it was day 91 on my AT hike (Early Riser Day 91). I only show one small section of the trail during my descent, as I rarely had enough calmness of mind to think about pulling out my camera to film. However, pay particular attention to my recap at the end of the day that starts around the 16:50 point in the video. I rarely show much emotion in my videos, but the look on my face as I discuss that descent tells it all. And that comes from a guy who used to jump 350-pound barrels out of airplanes at 13,000 feet and has been in numerous firefights against terrorists overseas. I can still remember the feeling of being terrified as I careened out of control toward that cliff. I never told my wife this story, and she will read it for the first time when she edits this chapter. That should be entertaining.

We often observe hikers on YouTube struggling to figure out how to establish the proper path and get their rider and elephant on board with the plan. I watched a clear example of this on a vlogger's video just recently where he started his northbound hike in early January on the AT. Not surprisingly, the temps were cold and there was snow and ice on the ground for the entire first week of his hike. From the southern terminus at Springer Mountain to Neel Gap some 30 miles later, his starting conditions were difficult . . . but not impossible if mentally prepared. In his videos, he was complaining of being cold at night and was worried his choice of sleep systems was not adequate for the conditions he was facing. He had a zero-degree sleeping bag, and the temps were hovering in the mid to low 20s at night. But he was still shivering and could not stay warm enough as he tried to sleep.

It's easy to imagine that his rider was probably working overtime attempting to find a solution to these chilly nights, and his elephant was likely injecting massive amounts of "We can't stay out here in these conditions; we are miserable and cold," thoughts in his head. We see this play out on his fourth night on trail when he stops at a shelter for the night and sets up his sleep system on the wooden floor of the structure. The problem with this becomes that the floors of these shelters are hollow underneath and the boards usually have gaps between them. This leaves you at the mercy of the icy wind blowing up through the shelter floor.

When he panned his camera around the shelter, you could see the snow on the ground through the boards he would sleep on. He did not place a protective layer down over the floor before placing his inflatable sleeping pad and sleeping bag down directly on the porous wood planks. It became immediately obvious why he had been shivering at night in a sleeping bag well suited for the temps he was experiencing. The worst part of the situation was that it was easily preventable.

Pro-tip: *For any newer hikers out there eyeing some time on the AT in the winter months, the basic rule is: Sleep in your tent when it's cold to maximize heat retention from your body and your sleep system. But if you decide to sleep in the shelter, place a protective layer down on the floor to not only block the air coming up from underneath but also to protect your air mattress from splinters and other puncture hazards.*

So, why did I use this example in a chapter about how to craft a path that caters to both your rider and your elephant? Well, it's easy to predict that he was not sleeping well at night which was robbing his rider of the rest it needed to problem-solve effectively. Additionally, his elephant was probably lobbing emotion-laden thoughts about how bad the cold sucks and how much better it would be if they just went back home and stopped this nonsense. In fact, we find out a few minutes later in the video that this was exactly what happened. He called his wife and told her to come get him because he was hanging it up. Five days into a hike he had prepared extremely hard for, and like countless others before him, he decided to hang it up just 30 miles in. However, as luck would have it, a veteran thru-hiker was working at Mountain Crossings (the store at Neel Gap) and nudged the hiker to stick with it for a little longer. He called his wife and told her not to come to get him because he was going to stay on trail for one more week and see where he was mentally after that.

Quick Aside: *He eventually hung up his hike around the 200-mile mark for various reasons. I applaud him for sticking with it and making it another 170 miles past Neel Gap. But my goal for this book is to help every one of you make it to your destination and not stop until you get there.*

The question we should ask is this: In that same situation, what could we do to prime our environment to keep our rider and elephant satiated and willing to move forward together? The answer is that we could remove the obstacle of getting little to no sleep by avoiding sleeping in shelters and choosing instead to pitch our tent to take advantage of the heat retention. Ahh, but you see, our elephants will try to convince us to take the path of least resistance. It nudges us to just sleep in the shelter because it would be much quicker to set up and pack up compared to pitching our tent. That System 1 part of our mind wants to employ the easiest solution and our System 2 is usually offline at the end of a hard hiking day and won't fight back. Our elephant's desire for ease and comfort will allow a very avoidable mistake to create one of the most destructive obstacles for a long-distance hiker—lack of sleep. By simply removing the obstacle of sleep deprivation, we increase our chance for success dramatically. By replenishing our mind and body with sleep's restorative powers, we are more likely to avoid the negative funnel of emotions that will convince us to end our hikes. We will discuss sleep in-depth in Chapter Eleven.

Hopefully, through these two examples, you can get the feel for how we can reduce some of the friction on our path as we push towards our long-distance hiking destinations. I also hope it's obvious that our biggest obstacle during our journey will be our elephant. Not to say that our rider won't have his moments; mine drives me crazy for sure. But when we think about tweaking our environment and building habits, we must keep the bulk of our efforts aimed at our elephant. Its conditioned behavior keeps it desiring convenience, comfort, and ease and will undoubtedly steer us off course very quickly. Just like your System 1 convinced you in less than a second that the ball in Chapter Two costs 10 cents, your elephant will convince you that its desires are the best decision for you in the moment. By simply having the awareness that this will happen during our hike, and by shaping our path to avoid the elephant winning the majority of these decisions, we have increased our chances of staying on trail exponentially.

Now that we have a better understanding of the two parts of our divided minds, and how to adjust the path in front of us, it's time to look at some common mental landmines that trigger our elephant and distract our rider. One of the most common and dangerous is the way we perceive the information pouring in through our senses. We can rarely separate ourselves from these perceptions as they happen. Understanding our brain's perceiving power can help us avoid unnecessary mental chaos and keep us pushing towards our goals.

Chapter Six
Perceptions

Perception is a mirror, not a fact. And what I look on is my state of mind, reflected outward.

Ralph Waldo Emerson

I cannot begin this chapter in any other fashion than to have you reread the above epigraph by Ralph Waldo Emerson. If you can grasp and internalize what he is saying, then you have a huge head start on where we are going in this chapter. If you can yield to the notion that what you see in this world is your interpretation of reality, not reality itself, then you have taken the first step to freeing yourself from your mind's false perceptions. How do we do this? By managing the gap between your interpretation of reality and reality itself. Confused? Let's dig deeper into this secret that touches every human on the planet.

Let's begin by trying to describe what I mean by "perception" in the context of this book. "Perception is the sensory experience of the world. It involves both recognizing environmental stimuli and actions in response to these stimuli."[7] "Perception acts as a filter that allows us to exist and interpret the world without becoming overwhelmed by the abundance of stimuli."[8] This last sentence is the critical piece of understanding the inaccuracy of our perceptions. It's a filter that interprets the world for us, so we don't have to use tons of conscious energy to sort out all the sensory data coming in.

It's our mental filters that present the biggest challenge with our perceptions. The unconscious parts of our minds control these autonomic—happening on their own outside of conscious awareness—filters. If you read my first book about the ego, then you know exactly what I am talking about here. Our filter (which the ego controls a substantial portion) is using our beliefs, values, concepts, expectations, knowledge, and experiences to create how we perceive the world. But it's not real, and all of us are creating our own fake little bubble around us and convincing ourselves that it's reality.

None of us are having the same experience. None of us perceive things exactly the same, and to be honest, none of us ever get to experience reality in its purest form. To put this into context, go to the following website https://en.wikipedia.org/wiki/The_dress (or just google the blue and black dress illusion) and describe the colors of the dress in the picture without reading anything about it first. Come back here when you have made your choice.

For those of you who are a bit lazy like me and didn't go look at the picture, what's shown is a striped dress comprised of two different colors. People viewing the dress fall into one of two camps: they either see the dress as black and blue or white and gold. Wait a minute, what? How can different people see such inconsistency in the colors of the same dress? For those of you who didn't go to the website, now is your chance. Go on. I know you want to.

When I view the dress, I see it as black and blue. There is none of the normal "Well, I can see how you might see it as some other colors." No, it's very clear to me that the dress is black and blue. I will concede that I see some noticeably light tinges of gold on the edges of the black stripes, but they are still clearly black.

Now, for all of those who see the dress as black and blue, you probably felt a sense of connection with me when I revealed my perception of the dress. However, my guess is that around half of you felt some internal dissonance when you realized I didn't see the dress the same way that you are perceiving it—as white and gold. I am sure you are just as convinced the dress is white and gold as I am it's black and blue. Somewhere deep inside, your elephant didn't enjoy feeling the incoherence between what you are so sure you are seeing compared to what I am telling you I am seeing. But here is the secret. This incongruence is happening all day, every day, in some fashion. We just fail to realize it because our perceptions and experiences feel so accurate and real to us. We don't question it because we assume it's reality and the same for everyone.

My son introduced me to this when he handed me his phone one evening and asked what color the striped dress was. Not thinking anything nefarious was at play, I quickly said black and blue and handed his phone back to him. Now, if you are like me, you may assume that since he is my offspring, we probably see the dress the same. Nope. He instantly retorted, "You're crazy, it's white and gold," and turned to walk out of my room. Perplexed, I had him come back so I could look at the picture again. Black and blue, just like I thought. I also thought that he must be messing with me, but as I researched it further, I found the Wikipedia article and read about the dress and the paradox. But you see, that is the whole point of this chapter.

Most of us perceive the world around us and automatically assume that we are seeing everything the way it truly is. That the people around us are perceiving everything the way we are. Hear me clearly . . . none of us are perceiving things exactly alike. We are all different in our own unique way. The cold, biting breeze is uncomfortable for some, while others are longing for the same breeze to cool them down after a tough climb up a steep mountain. It's all coming through our filters, and we are at the mercy of our elephant who is at the controls of our perception levers. A horde of New England black flies can be maddening for many, yet to others, the flies offer no frustration at all. It's all in how you allow yourself to perceive it. I hope that the dress example will nudge you off your perch of normalcy and comfort. That it will make your System 2 brain wake up and make you more curious about why you are perceiving things the way you do.

A Quick Aside For Einstein

If you are still struggling with this concept, maybe a thought from one of the most brilliant and curious men in history can help. Albert Einstein was not only a gifted physicist, but he also philosophized about the surrounding universe. His nonstop curiosity sparked his rider into action and ensured his elephant didn't get the final vote in all his decisions. His curious nature led him to the discovery of the fundamental choice that shapes our perceptions and our life. *"The most important decision we make is whether we believe we live in a friendly or hostile universe."* It's a choice that each of us must make for ourselves, but we mustn't forget that our conditioned mind is making this choice for us . . . until we can wake up enough to realize what is happening.

For 40 years I believed (at the unconscious elephant level) that the universe was a hostile entity and everything in life oriented against me and my survival. Why does this matter? Because our perceptions of life run through this filter and if we believe negativity surrounds us, then our perceptions of the things happening in our lives will ALWAYS have a negative hue to them. In each experience, we will be more apt to find the threat and miss the splendor. Instead of soaking in the beauty of a great conversation, we walk away worrying about how stupid we sounded and that they must think we are an idiot. Instead of seeing the beauty surrounding us on our climb up the steep mountain, we keep looking ahead for the peak, wishing we were already there so the pain and torture will end. That's why I think Einstein's universe decision is more profound than any of his other theories. It's a simple choice that will drive how we perceive life in every second we are alive.

If we can shift to the belief that the universe is friendly, then we enable ourselves to find the good in each experience. Failures turn into learning opportunities, we stop harboring ill feelings towards others, we can see the internal beauty in everyone, we learn to release negativity and hold on to positivity, and we learn to savor each step of our journey because the magnificence of the moment is pouring into our senses.

Back on Path

As we move forward and begin discussing how this applies to a long-distance hiker, I want to distance us from the very physical experience of the black and blue dress (yes, the dress is actually black and blue). Although it's a good way to introduce you to the world of differing perceptions, what we will talk about in this chapter won't be as obvious or tangible. For example, if you and I were hiking together on the AT and you pointed out an interesting tree or flower, I will see these objects mostly the same. I am not suggesting that we are all having a completely different visual or auditory experience, but I am nudging you to realize that my mind is not the same place as your mind when we are experiencing the same sensory input. It's our internal environment in these moments, combined with our past experiences, that are creating the gap between what I perceive and what you perceive. It's in those differences that we often get lost. We feel like we are having the "real" experience and can't figure out why the other person is seeing it so incorrectly.

In reality, the differences in perception that you have with other hikers won't matter much on trail unless it somehow creates friction and suffering for one or both of you. However, what I am pushing you to consider is that your perception of the world around you will be a critical piece in your journey. Your perceptions drive your overall experience. The beautiful part is that you get to choose how you perceive the world. Unfortunately, most of us remain blind to how our unconscious conditioning is pulling our perception levers without our conscious consent. We just keep running the same scripts that feel comfortable but may not serve our journey or our goals.

Far too often I get sucked into the negative side of perception for absolutely no reason, other than it's a habitual process that I don't control during most moments of the day. But this is where our rider can employ his skills to help us if we can become aware of the gap between our perception and reality. Inside this gap lies the opportunity to nudge our elephant to find the good in each moment. To bring its powerful emotional tools to bear and help us experience the universe in its natural state, without all the unnecessary junk we pile on top of it. Let's look at how our rider and elephant are involved in this process of perception so we can figure out how to gain some agency over it.

The elephant is probably the easier of the two to describe. When I say easier, I mean in the sense that the elephant's filters are the scripts we have been building (mostly unconsciously) our entire lives. These scripts were created from the experiences with our parents, grandparents, siblings, friends, watching television, time spent on social media, our community, our culture, and the list goes on and on. The most important thing to realize is that the elephant's filters are automatic, instinctive, and are hard to interrupt or shape without our rider being very conscious in the moments between the sensory input and the perception created by our elephant. Unless we can become conscious of how our elephant's filters are processing the sensory data coming in, then we will always be at the mercy of the scripts that are hard-baked inside us . . . whether they serve us positively or not.

Since our experiences created these scripts, they make it feel like most things we experience in the world are aimed at us, or at least affect us in some manner. It creates a perception bubble around us. Therefore, as we move down the trail and things enter our bubble, we relate them to us. The hidden root I just stubbed my toe on becomes something I take personally. The wetness of the trail soaks my shoes, and my wet feet make it feel like the trail is deliberately trying to make my hike harder. As you feel your feet get wetter and wetter, the headline that makes it to your consciousness goes something like this: "Ugh . . . if I hike with these wet shoes on all day, I will get blisters or trench foot." You see, it's our elephant's emotional, automatic reactions to the stimuli during our hike that creates the chaos in our minds, not the stimuli itself.

By the way, why are wet feet such a negative perception for hikers? I bet more energy is wasted by hikers trying to keep their feet dry than any other problem confronting us on trail. Some hikers act like their wet shoes are going to rot their feet off by day's end, not considering that people that hike the Florida Trail are wading in water for days on end with little ill effect on their feet. My question remains, Why? Why do people think if they hike all day with wet feet, they will come down with trench foot or some other debilitating condition? It's ridiculous really but highlights how much our elephant's filter is tainting the beautiful data entering our senses with fears of unfounded nonsense.

Let's put this into a hiking context that most of us have experienced. If you walk upon a campsite on trail and become enraged when you see trash left in the firepit, then your elephant just filtered your sensory data into a negative experience. The headline that got pushed to your conscious mind would probably go something like this: "I can't believe someone would be so insensitive that they would leave a bunch of plastic inside the firepit for others to clean up." You didn't get a vote in the outrage. Your elephant took your values and previous experiences and compared them to the visual input of the trash in the firepit . . . and anger soon followed.

Example from Social Media

Interestingly, I just read a comment on a hiking Facebook page where a female replied to a post about someone leaving trash at a campsite. Her reply read, "The people that do that aren't hikers, they are invaders!" Umm . . . OK, I guess, but that sure sounds like her elephant triggered her negative emotions towards something she has absolutely no control over. And whether we want to admit it or not, that outrage is a worthless waste of energy. David Eagleman said it best in his book *The Brain*, when he stated, "You don't perceive objects as they are. You perceive them as you are."[9] Therefore, whatever joy, love, hate, or turmoil you have swirling inside you will become the filters your brain uses when perceiving the surrounding environment. I am guessing the "invaders" comment mentioned above didn't come from an internal filter of joy, love, and compassion . . . but maybe that's my own filter creating a perception and clouding my judgment.

Back on Path

Please don't take this as an indictment of your value system. I get it, people that leave trash in nature piss me off too. But here's the secret: Your elephant's script sent you into a conditioned perception that has now become a negative obstruction in your mental space. Sure, you can let your emotions run wild and convince yourself that being passionate about "leave no trace" serves some higher good . . . but look around. There is no one here but you. Who is your anger helping at that moment? The offender is long gone and living their own life. Your negative emotions release the cocktail of stress hormones (cortisol and adrenalin) into

YOUR system, not the offender's system. YOU are the only one left suffering from someone else's actions.

Your elephant was triggered, and it felt so comfortable that you went all in without realizing it was happening. Instead of viewing your two options from an unemotional state, you jumped straight to mental suffering. However, what we fail to realize is that we are still left with the same two choices: either pick the trash up and carry it out with us or leave the trash behind because the next garbage can might be days away. When we let our elephant (and our ego) have free rein on creating our perceptions, we take things personally and create suffering in our minds . . . for absolutely no benefit whatsoever.

Reaching back to my experience in The Whites, this next example happened just two days after my crazy downclimb on the north side of Mount Moosilauke. It was a sunny and cold day, and the biting wind was brutal as I traversed across the infamous Franconia Ridge. I later made it over Mount Garfield and South Twin Mountain as I plodded my way towards the Zealand Falls Hut, where I would stealth camp for the night. However, about six miles shy of the hut, I ran into a multi-mile section of trail that was still covered in deep snow.

The temperature in this section was well above freezing and the monorail—a narrow line of snow that is compacted and firm, making hiking much easier if you walk on top of it—was getting soft and collapsing. This meant that every time I took a step, each foot would do one of three things: 1) find a somewhat firm surface and only sink a couple of inches (rare); 2) find a soft surface and sink several feet (40 percent of the time); 3) slide off the side of the collapsing monorail causing me to fall sideways as my foot kept sinking until my crotch hit the snow and stopped the descent (50 percent of the time). It made the next few hours tremendously challenging. Not only because of the extreme physical hardship from the snow but because I quickly realized I wouldn't make my camp spot before dark.

As I kept taking the next step and sinking into the deep snow, my elephant became more and more triggered. In fact, I was in the biggest mental hell I had experienced in a long time. I was already exhausted from walking over several mountains and just wanted to set up my tent, eat, and go to sleep. But now, I was making less than a half-mile an hour and was becoming exhausted to the point where I started considering turning around and heading back to the last hut. Going backward is something I abhor and won't do unless it becomes a life-or-death situation (and then . . . only maybe).

My perception at that moment equaled misery, pain, and suffering to a maximum level and there was no sign of it ending anytime soon. But then I heard it. I heard what sounded like someone coming towards me from the opposite direction. I thought to myself that I must be hearing things because nobody would be out in this section walking southbound and suffering voluntarily in this deep snow hell. But then Nate came around the next turn and I could see by the look on his face that he recognized me. I greeted him and he said, "I came to bring you your Cherry Coke." (Thanks again Nate! You are amazing!)

There's a back story to why he came to give me this soda, but it's not important here. The main takeaway is that the perception I had created for myself during this afternoon of hiking was one of hell and suffering. Nate, on the other hand, was in a great mental state and was having a good time hiking in the snow. You can watch a piece of our interaction on the Day 94 video of my AT Thru-Hike vlog on YouTube (timestamp 8:30). How could two people in the same place and time be having such a different experience? Ralph Waldo Emerson gave us the hint: *"Perception is a mirror, not a fact. And what I look on is my state of mind, reflected outward."*

After we talked for a few minutes and then went our separate ways, I was still creating a mental hell for myself as the deep snow continued (even though I was energized by the sugar in the Cherry Coke). But what I was left with after the interaction with Nate was the realization that he was having a completely different experience than I was, even though we were in the same conditions. He was perceiving the day as a positive experience, and I had created a mental hell for myself. His elephant seemed to be pumping positive emotions like awe and gratitude into his system, while mine injected self-doubt, stress, and misery.

Over the next few miles, I passed several more day hikers who were all enthusiastic and seemed to be having the time of their lives. They too were grateful to be in those beautiful mountains and didn't seem to let the deep snow affect them in the least. My negative emotions were so visceral that I can still remember how they felt as I write this four years later. However, the positive outcome of the experience became a signpost to how destructive my perceptions can be if I let my mind run loose.

Hopefully, I have helped you realize how your elephant will be triggered when something you experience violates your values or expectations. Luckily, there is a tiny gap between our uptake of sensory stimuli and the elephant's triggered emotions. Inside this gap is where the rider can help us choose a better path.

So how do we prevent our perceptions from injecting obstacles in our path on trail? Here is a technique that every hiker (and human) can use to reframe those moments when we feel our experience is taking a negative turn.

Imagine the scene you are in, but without you in it. For example: If you are on a muddy section of trail in Vermont, it's pouring rain, and you keep sinking into the deep mud on every step, just stop for a minute and create that scene in your mind exactly as it is, but without you in it. How do things change? Is the trail still muddy? Is the standing water covering the trail still present? Are the bugs still swarming? Is the rain still falling on everything in the scene? Are the sounds of nature still taking place? Of course they are. All these things are still happening and our presence has absolutely no meaning to this scene whatsoever. It would all take place without us present.

By asking ourselves these questions, we create that gap between reality and our perception. Reality finds the universe carrying out its existence in its most perfect form. The rain is its way of maintaining life for the planet. The mud is just a beautiful concoction created from the rain mixing with the soil that has formed from millions of years of decaying plant life and other organisms. The bugs are nature's way of feeding other creatures. The standing water is a seasonal water source for all the creatures in the area. It's all PERFECT! Until we make it imperfect inside our minds.

When we pull ourselves out of the picture and look at true reality, what we are observing is beyond description. If I gave you a magic wand and unlimited wishes, I argue you couldn't create a world so incredibly diverse and self-sustaining as the one we inhabit. But then we plug ourselves back into the scene and suddenly we perceive this world like we are at the center. Like everything is happening to us, instead of just happening. Therefore, we suffer, and it's only when we can manage the gap between reality and our perception of reality that we can let go of our ridiculous belief that we are at the center of anything.

When I'm on my hiking journey and it storms really hard, or the snow and ice are making traveling difficult, or my left knee is aching badly on the downhills, I have two choices: I can let my elephant turn the sensory data entering my nervous system into a narrative that places me at the center of the experience (which leads to mental suffering), or I can use the talents of my rider to manage the gap between reality and perception by removing the "me" from the scene and see reality for what it is—a perfect harmony created by the universe. Einstein's friendly universe at its finest.

Does this mean that the path won't be wet and muddy anymore? Or that the bugs won't attack me relentlessly? Or that the lack of rain won't make managing my water much harder in the extreme heat? Of course not, but if I can train my rider to inject himself in the gap, I can change my perception from being a victim to just simply being. I can see reality a little clearer and avoid letting my elephant send me down an instant path of suffering. I can let my rider manage the reality-perception gap and use the elephant in more beneficial ways, like generating the positive emotions of awe and gratitude. If our rider can nudge the elephant into unleashing its positive emotional power, then there is no obstacle we can't overcome. Let's look at a few tactical ways to nudge our elephant towards the positive path in front of us.

As you will hear me say repeatedly, unleashing our elephant's positive emotions is the most potent tool we have for removing obstacles and keeping our forward momentum. Emotions like gratitude and awe can inject powerful chemicals into our system and help buffer the negative effects of the stress our autonomic mind creates organically.

Gratitude is a powerful emotional trigger that releases dopamine and serotonin. These two neurotransmitters help to engender a positive and empathetic mood and help to nudge us towards enjoyment and away from suffering. It's a quick and easy means of changing how we are seeing things inside our perception bubble. We will discuss gratitude in more detail later in the book, but just realize, we all need more gratitude in our lives, starting this very moment. Spend a second and offer yourself some gratitude for reading this book and preparing your mind for your own long journey. You are right where you are supposed to be.

Experiencing awe is also a powerful trigger for positive emotions. Awe is that feeling we experience when confronted with something greater than the self.[10] On trail, this can be as simple as an expansive view from a mountain top, walking through a unique section of forest, seeing a massive oak tree that is hundreds of years old, drinking from a spring coming out of the side of a mountain, and millions of other moments that make us stop in our tracks and experience the magical world around us. These moments make us realize we are just a tiny speck inside this massive universe and helps us break free of our perception bubble. It helps us perceive the world without our filter turned on high.

Studies reveal that awe releases dopamine (neurotransmitter) and oxytocin (fast-acting hormone).[11] The benefit for us is that these chemicals prime us for pro-social behavior and altruism. In other words, it reduces our focus on ourselves and aims our focus on connecting with and helping things outside of our little perception bubble. It helps us realize we are not a separate entity in this experience. That we are part of the unified whole.

Awe helps to dampen our ego and increase our sense of connectedness with the universe. Best of all, it is free and available to us whenever we need it. This awareness hit me hard during my 113 days on the AT. I realized I didn't need to see expansive views or reach some big milestone to experience awe. Everything surrounding me on trail was a true miracle of creation. But why did it take me going on a long-distance journey to realize this again? How have humans grown so numb to this world that we aren't walking around in a constant state of awe?

Now, I know some of you are thinking this is getting a bit mystical, yet I would bet a paycheck that every single person reading this book has experienced awe hundreds of times throughout your life. I argue that the allure of awe draws many towards an adventure like a long-distance hike. We want to unplug from the Matrix and experience emotions like awe and gratitude. We want to find our gratefulness for the gifts the universe is presenting us. In doing so, we can disrupt the negative perceptions that plague our elephant's conditioned thoughts. We can teach ourselves how to be more still and view the world around us in a more positive light.

The last tip I will offer in this chapter is a strategy one of my peers at work shared during a training course for our elite operators. The phrase "I get to" versus "I have to" hit me like a ton of bricks when I heard it. I am not sure why it sent me into such an awakening inside my mind, but when I heard this simple concept, I could reflect through my life and see all the mornings where I climbed out of bed to face the day because it felt like I had to. All the mornings I dreaded going to work because I had to. All the miles of running on the soft sand in the Marine Corps because I had to. Leaving my family for the seventh deployment because I had to.

If you want to see what self-created suffering looks like up close, simply watch your natural reactions to things you perceive as non-enjoyable or taxing. What's your elephant's reaction when you are tired after a long week at work, but you must get up on Saturday to do several hours of yard work? How does your elephant react when you wake up in your tent and feel extremely groggy and sore, but you have to hike 15 miles to get into town to grab your resupply box before the post office closes at noon? What is your elephant's reaction when the trail turns into a muddy swamp first thing in the morning, and it forces you to walk in wet, muddy shoes the rest of the day?

We all have different things that trigger our elephant's negative perceptions. Once triggered, the cascade of negative emotions will often follow us throughout our day. Depending on the severity of the situation, some of these emotions stay with us for much longer. However, once I learned the strategy of "I get to" versus "I have to," I gained the ability to adjust my elephant's perceptions before they sent me down the negativity funnel. My rider could inject this phrase in those moments where I felt the elephant's perceptions trend towards the negative.

When we change our script to "I get to," then we see everything we do as a blessing. Getting out from under the warm covers on a frigid morning becomes a positive event. Not because I don't feel the cold air making my fingers hurt as I roll up my tent, but because I am still alive and able to FEEL things like the cold on my skin. Every second is a gift. Everything that pours into our senses is a gift. Wet shoes are a gift. Cold rain is a gift. Yardwork is a gift. The fact that I have a box of goodies waiting on me at the post office is a gift. Each blaze you pass is a gift. The crotch-deep snow is a gift. But these are only gifts if we can train our minds to see them as gifts. Try the phrase "I get to" in all facets of your life, but especially when you get out on trail. I can assure you it will help refocus some of our self-generated sufferings into positive experiences. The universe is creating this experience for you. Don't let your conditioned mind disrupt the beauty of the experience.

Chapter Seven
The Danger of Expectations

> *Expectation feeds frustration. It is an unhealthy attachment to people, things, and outcomes we wish we could control . . . but don't.*
>
> Steve Maraboli

If forced to rate the top mental obstacle long-distance hikers create for themselves, the choice would be easy—expectations. Whether it's what they expect from their hike before they start, or what they expect over the next few days on trail, expectations distract our rider and trigger our elephant . . . for little to no value at all. Believe me, I get it. I am an expectation-creating beast. I have been this way my entire life. It shouldn't come as a surprise that my life has also been filled with an immense amount of mental suffering. I don't mean suffering in some very perceptible ways. No, I am talking about the "death from a thousand cuts" type of suffering that hides just below the radar of our consciousness.

It was all the little things that didn't match my expectations that created the most chaos in my mind. The times that reality didn't play out the way I expected. My inability to handle the discord between what I expected to happen and what actually happened caused mental suffering on a repetitive loop. Let's use an example from my Marine Recon days to illustrate what we are talking about here.

My eight-man team was tasked to conduct a reconnaissance training mission inside the ranges of Camp Lejeune, North Carolina, where I was stationed at the time. It was early spring, and the weather called for a 40 percent chance of rain each of the four days we would be in the field. In my head, a 40 percent chance of rain equaled the hope that it wouldn't rain on us while we were out there. I knew if it did, I would be wet, cold, and miserable with no hope of a reprieve during the patrol. I kept reminding myself that we had a 60 percent chance of not suffering, and my elephant went all-in on those odds.

Fortunately, the first two days met my expectations as we avoided any serious rain. It sprinkled a bit during the second day but not enough to matter. However, the last two days turned into what felt like a tropical depression hanging directly over our team and soaked us to the bone. Over those excruciating 48 hours, I spent most of them in my head wallowing in misery. Why? Because I had expected the training patrol to be fun, exciting, and mostly dry. Not wet, cold, and miserable to a maximum degree.

I was in a mental prison and lacked the tools to gain awareness of my predicament or to get myself out. Eating was hard in the rain, sleeping was impossible, and the mosquitos came out in droves. Just so I'm painting a clear picture here for those of you unfamiliar with life on a reconnaissance patrol, there are no tents, fires, or camping when you're in the field. When bad weather hits, you're like a horse in the rain . . . you just have to sit there and take it.

As the last morning broke ever so slowly on the horizon, we huddled together, waiting to be extracted by a Marine Corps CH-

46 helicopter via SPIE (Special Patrol Insertion Extraction) method. For those unfamiliar, this method uses a long rope that hangs underneath the helicopter. Each Marine dons a harness on the outside of their uniform that allows them to connect to the SPIE line safely. Once overhead, the helicopter lowers the SPIE line to the ground, and we hook ourselves in. Once hooked in, the helicopter lifts us out of the forest and we fly dangling from the rope to a safe landing zone outside of the simulated enemy territory. It was a freaking exciting way to end the training, but now I expected it to be a torturous flight because of the frigid temperatures that had befallen us. The cold front had moved through and the temps had dropped into the mid-40s. Worst of all, we were all soaking wet from the last 48 hours of rain.

I remember looking around at the misery on my teammates' faces as we sat in our patrol base pulling security. Seven of the hardest men I had ever met were alone inside their private mental prisons. We were all suffering at levels we had never experienced before, and that says a lot for Marines who had already been through reconnaissance selection and training. But then it happened.

For a reason that I can't recall now, all eight of us looked at each other and were suddenly freed from our mental prisons. We looked into each other's eyes and began smiling. For the first time in hours, our minds shifted from our selfish misery to the shared experience we were having with each other. Once connected mentally, our entire world changed. We let go of our expectations and embraced the present moment. Sure, it was cold (we were all shivering so hard we were jack hammering) and everything we had was soaked to the core, but we still had so much to be grateful for. We still had each other, and we embraced this lifestyle together. It was a brotherhood bolstered by tough men living through tough experiences.

Not long after, we heard the blades of our extraction helicopter getting closer and we smiled even more. We donned our harnesses and moved tactically to the edge of the clearing. As the helicopter pilot lowered the SPIE line, we raced to our positions and snapped ourselves in. We were soon hanging 300 feet over the swamps of Camp Lejeune, flying at speeds that felt extremely fast to the wet and weary Marines hanging below the helicopter. I could see the faces of the guys above and below me, and it was evident they were having the time of their lives. They weren't in their mental hell anymore, and neither was I. Even though the wind chill from our forward movement had to be well below freezing, we felt none of it. We were free from those imprisoning expectations and living in the present moment. It was an experience that will live with me until death.

From this example, there were two moments when I set mental expectations for the future. The first was the hope that we would remain relatively rain-free during our patrol, and the second was that the ride on the SPIE line was going to be miserable. These expectations created a mental future in my mind that snowballed into misery and suffering. When my "it's not going to rain" expectation was destroyed by 48 hours of downpours, I suffered immeasurably. When I predicted that the SPIE extraction would be miserable because of the cold, I sat there mentally suffering in the hours leading up to the helicopter arriving for exfil. But that expectation didn't manifest either. Our expectations are rarely accurate, yet we keep creating them repeatedly in our minds. It's the perfect example of our rider trying to predict future outcomes and our elephant injecting its emotional responses to these predictions.

I think about my time in the military a lot when the subject of expectations comes up. I was blind to the fact that I was the one causing the suffering. It wasn't the environment, the people around me, or bad luck ghosting me like a shadow. It was simply my habit of setting expectations that would incite mental suffering when they failed to manifest as desired. Instead of setting the expectation that I should just flow with life and be malleable in the face of hardship, I created a red line of hope that would leave me in a mental prison when things didn't play out as expected.

As I grew older, and maybe a bit wiser, I decided to thru-hike the Appalachian Trail. I placed myself back into an arena where I would get to test my ability to let go of expectations and try to stay in the present moment. I wanted to see if I could let go of my tendency to create a personal mental prison. Was I successful? Hardly, but I damn sure became more aware of what was happening and how my elephant was manifesting the suffering in my mind. The most important lesson I learned during those 2,200 miles was the realization that I was not the center of the experience I was having.

I know this concept will push many of you to wonder what in the hell I am talking about. Most of us live our entire lives staring out from behind our eyes, absorbing the world through our senses, and feeling like we are the center of our experience. It's the only way our minds can make sense of the world, even though it's patently false. Hear me clearly . . . NOTHING is centered on us. NOTHING!

To think we are at the center of our experience will create a mental model in our heads that leaves us feeling like things are happening to us instead of simply happening. "The rain that is falling on me is the universe's way of getting back at me for something I did in the past." "The steep trail up the mountain was someone's attempt at making me hate hiking; why couldn't they just put more switchbacks to make it easier?" "The pain in my body is much worse than what others experience at this point in their hike." "My journey to Katahdin is harder than what others experienced." "Not many hikers before me had to deal with this much cold, rain, snow, heat, bugs, blah, blah, blah."

Let me put it this way so we are all on the same sheet of music. This type of thinking is 100 percent worthless and the person running these scripts in your head is a phony narrator of false stories. Most humans aren't aware that this "I am the center of my experience" charade is creating suffering in their lives. However, if we can shine the light of awareness on this charade long enough, we can start to see it's not about us. It's much, much, bigger than us.

History can often be our greatest source of awareness. As an example, there was a moment in time when man discovered the earth was not the center of the universe. Prior to this historical event, it was the common belief that the sun, moon, planets, and stars all revolved around their center point—the earth. However, one night in 1610, an astronomer named Galileo gazed through his homemade telescope and realized that the moons of Jupiter were revolving around Jupiter, not around the earth. Imagine that for a second, throughout all recorded history, mankind was categorically convinced they were the center of all existence—until Galileo proved it was all nonsense. He proved it isn't about us. He proved it's so much bigger than any of us.

Fast forward to our current context, and I'm now pushing all of us to realize the same thing about ourselves—that we are not at the center of this amazing occurrence we call life. We are simply an infinitesimal piece of the grand experience that is taking place in the universe, and none of it is centered on us. To add context to how insignificant we are to the universe, Brian Greene, a theoretical physicist at Columbia University, stated that if you "Hold your thumb at arm's length against the night sky, it will cover more than 10 million galaxies in the observable universe."[12] That's so freaking hard for me to grasp . . . 10 million galaxies that are similar in size to the massive galaxy we live in. And that's just one tiny portion of the expansive night sky above us. Again, we are the center of nothing.

Why does this matter? How does it harm anything if I consider myself the center of the experience I am having? The answers to these two questions are important if we want to free ourselves from the suffering of our expectations.

When we place ourselves as the star in the center of our experience, we inadvertently create an excess of unrealistic expectations. We center these expectations around how "we" think things should be to ensure "we" have the best experience possible. We eventually forget that "we" are just a grain of sand in the proverbial desert of the universe.

Many of you reading this might want to push back against the accusation that you're selfish, simply because you feel you are the center of your experience. This internal friction is the key. Remember, this is about biology, not personality. Biology doesn't care about our feelings. The truth of our biology is that we are all selfish at a primordial level. Our brains are wired to survive. To do this, we are always unconsciously trying to create an environment around us that allows the best chance to survive and procreate. Therefore, we are wired to consider ourselves in a way that feels like we are the center of our experience. You are hopefully not selfish in a personality kind of way, but you are selfish in a homo sapiens kind of way. We all share this biology, and it's why we set expectations that are anchored with us at the center of the experience. We live in our heads 24/7. It feels like everything is happening to us, but we must expand our awareness to see the truth.

We forget that the rain is falling on everything around us . . . not just us. We forget that the frigid temperatures would be the same whether we are on this trail or not. We forget that the water source was dry for everyone in desperate need of water, not just us. We forget that the hordes of black flies are just a beautiful creation of nature and don't exist to turn our hike into a medieval torture session. We forget that the seven other guys are suffering just as badly as we are in the cold rain. Let's look at a few of the more common expectations hikers set for themselves on trail.

A lot of aspiring thru-hikers expect to have some kind of spiritual journey on trail. But what happens when their hike starts feeling like work and not a journey of finding oneself? What happens when they are deep into their hike and feel no closer to finding themselves than when they started? What happens when they start feeling even more confused about their post-trail life?

Other hikers set expectations of hiking slowly so they can smell the roses. But what happens when they are weighed down with eight days of food as they leave each town because it takes them so long to reach the next resupply point? How will that extra weight compound the punishment on their body and mind as they are "hiking slow and enjoying it?" What happens when their extended hiking time leaves them enduring more days of foul weather and spending more money to finance the extra days on trail?

Other hikers expect to find a tramily (trail family) to link up with and enjoy the fellowship of other hikers on their long journey. But what happens when they can't seem to keep pace with the hikers they want to latch onto? What happens when they find themselves alone for the majority of their hike? What happens when the loneliness becomes overwhelming?

As William Shakespeare stated, "Expectation is the root of all heartache," and this is a stark reality on a long-distance hike for sure. However, if it's so obvious that setting expectations will only bring us heartache, then why are we so blind to the fact that we do it to ourselves? If we want to have the best chance of finishing these long-distance hikes, then we must figure out a way to turn down the volume on the expectation settings in our minds. We must learn to let go of the shore and let the universe's current carry us along. How can we do this, you ask?

I suggest it's about focusing our rider's attention on the right spots. Let's use the words of the great Stoic Epictetus to illuminate where our rider's focus should aim. "The chief task in life is simply this:

to identify and separate matters so that I can say clearly to myself which are externals not under my control and which have to do with the choices I actually control. Where then do I look for good and evil? Not to uncontrollable externals, but within myself to the choices that are my own… "[13]

Most of our expectations become this entangled mix of things under our control and things that aren't. If I expect to hike the Great Smoky Mountains section of the AT in 3.5 days (71 miles of tough hiking), then I have just inadvertently included many variables that I have no control over. What happens when it snows, and my pace slows to one mile an hour? What happens when the rain is so heavy that I am literally walking through a stream instead of a trail? What happens when the elevation and terrain wreck my body because of the ruggedness the Smokies are known for? What happens when a fire breaks out and they close a section of trail? What's the one thing we can predict once the uncontrollable variables start wreaking havoc on our expectations? You guessed it, mental suffering at its finest.

As things start going sideways in the Smokies, your rider will become consumed with solving problems that have no solutions because he controls very few of the variables. Your elephant will become triggered when it realizes you won't make it to your resupply point at Standing Bear Hostel on the fourth day. When both the rider and the elephant are focused on the wrong things, you can bet your path will be full of self-inflicted obstacles. These obstacles will frustrate your elephant and he will blame everything external to you, even though it's the internal you that is creating all the chaos. But, again, what is the solution? Epictetus revealed it to us. We must focus on the things we control and let go of any dissonance that arises from variables outside of our control.

We must narrow our rider's focus down to the internal variables we have control over, no matter what chaos is happening outside of us. We must remember that we control our perceptions. A quote I lean on to remind me of this comes from John Milton's poem "Paradise Lost," where he states, "The mind is its own place, and in itself can make a heaven of hell, a hell of heaven."[14] This simply reminds me that any experience I am having can either feel like heaven, or feel like hell, but the one commonality is that I control the narrative. If it feels like hell, it's because I allowed it to be that way.

In addition to our perceptions, we can control our attitude during each moment of the day. We can control our nutrition and hydration plan so we don't undermine our mental capacities by robbing our bodies of fuel, electrolytes, and water. We can control when we start and end our hike for the day. We can control putting earplugs in before we fall asleep so we get better rest and recovery at night. The point here is we have control over many variables on our hikes. If we focus on those, we can prevent our rider from getting sucked into giant problems he can't solve. We can prevent our elephant from getting triggered and creating emotional storms inside us. We can reduce the friction on the path ahead simply by focusing on the things we can control.

Our rider can't solve the 2,050 miles we have left to Katahdin, but he can solve making it to the next water source and cameling up. Our elephant stays triggered when we face discomfort and pain, but we can keep him satiated if we reach small goals during the day and reward our efforts (something as simple as a candy bar or listening to podcasts are the rewards I use for myself during the day). The most important point here is that if we continue to set expectations before and during our hike, we increase the risk of creating a hell of the heaven inside our experience . . . and none of us want that.

To round out this chapter on expectations, here is my advice for those who are about to undergo some type of long-duration event like a thru-hike. Don't set expectations for what you assume it will be like before and during the event. The truth is, there's no real way to know, and that's part of the magic. Setting expectations is the fastest way to find suffering. These long-duration events are hard enough without undermining our success by creating mental obstacles in our path.

Direct your rider to narrow his focus on what's right in front of you and keep your goals small and attainable. Focus on the bright spots during your day and build on them. Keep the elephant motivated by reaching the small goals you set and rewarding yourself for doing so. Use gratitude in the present moment to allow your elephant's emotional strengths to flood your body and mind. And last, but not least, expect nothing and appreciate everything. The universe owes us nothing but gives us everything if we are open and willing to accept it. Everything is perfect in its own way. Our task is to open our minds and simply flow with the experience the universe is crafting for us.

Chapter Eight
Fear and Clinging

The past is not clinging to you; YOU are clinging to the past. Once you are not clinging, the past simply evaporates.

Rajneesh

I look forward to delivering this chapter on fear and clinging because it's going to push many of you, and me for that matter, out of your comfort zone. I argue it's our natural habit of clinging to the objects in our lives that leads to much of the suffering we experience. The uncertainties we confront on trail, especially in the initial stages, amplifies our felt need to cling harder to the certainties in our life.

Since all this is happening in our System 1 elephant brain, we remain unconscious of our clinging tendencies. We remain blind to the fact that we are clinging to these items not out of fear of losing them per se, but the fear of losing ourselves. This fear creates the perception that we must hold on to these items for dear life. If I lose them, the definition of "me" may leave with them. Without them, who am I? This vicious circle ensures that we continue to cling to things in our life, whether they are good for us or not. Our elephant can't imagine losing the normalcy and comfort it has grown used to. It defines who we know as us.

How does this clinging happen in the first place? It starts with us uploading millions of bits of sensory information from our environment every second of the day. As the information comes streaming through our senses, our elephant brain filters the incoming data immediately. The problem is that the elephant uses much of our past pain, fear, shame, anger, and sadness as the filter. It's checking to see if anything entering looks, feels, smells, sounds, or tastes like something that caused us harm in the past. And it's doing all of this with no conscious involvement from us.

It's important to remember that our ancient elephant brain can't see into the future and is focused on our survival in the present moment. Therefore, he is looking for cues in the environment that may threaten our survival. If we see or hear something that resembles a rattlesnake, our elephant brain will immediately trigger a reaction. If we smell or taste the same type of food that made us sick previously, our elephant brain will trigger nausea so we don't make the same mistake again.

When I came down with the norovirus just north of Damascus, Virginia, the last thing I had eaten before throwing up violently was a PayDay candy bar. My brain made it impossible for me to eat another PayDay for the rest of my thru-hike, and it's making me a bit nauseous to think about it right now. The point is, we are unconsciously assessing our environment for all the things that may hurt us.

Our elephant isn't the only one scanning for threats; our rider creates a lot of the fear and anxiety we experience as well. Wired to look ahead and predict the future, our rider uses our past filters as the foundation for his prediction analysis. He scans ahead to see if any scenario in the future resembles experiences from the past that caused us pain and suffering.

Example: If you feel awkward around a lot of people, your rider is scanning ahead to ensure you don't get trapped in a situation where you are forced to be around a gathering of hikers—like at a shelter on the AT or a hostel in town. Or, the opposite can be true also. If you fear being alone, then your rider is looking at all future options to ensure you are around other hikers when bedding down for the night.

Since uncertainty abounds during a thru-hike, and our rider and elephant often measure events through a filter of fear, these combine to create a maelstrom of anxiety inside our minds. Dr. Jud Brewer, a neuroscientist at Brown University, has created this simple formula to help describe how our brain creates the anxiety many of us are plagued with. Fear + Uncertainty = Anxiety.[15] Now, insert this formula inside a long-distance hike (or any challenging long-duration event) and you can see why upwards of 75 percent of people drop off trail before reaching their original goal. These experiences are Petri dishes for anxiety to grow and thrive if we don't have the tools to prevent it from taking control of our mental landscape.

There isn't much certainty on the path ahead when hiking a long trail, and this seems to magnify the fears inside our minds. Fear of the dark, fear of being alone, fear of bears, fear of being hungry, fear of a tree falling on us as we sleep in our tents, fear of being cold, fear of being caught in a thunderstorm, fear of some crazy person hurting us, and the list could go on forever. Our rider is trying to look ahead and guide us down the proper path, but all he can often see is fear and uncertainty. The filter he uses to perceive the world creates much of the fear and clinging in our lives. When we are uncertain about what's next, we cling harder to what we have. It's biology at work to keep us alive. I have a much greater chance of surviving if I stay in a place that has proven to keep me comfortable and safe.

Fear is a powerful motivator, and we dislike letting go of things that feel safe in our ancient brain. When things stay stable and constant, our elephant doesn't experience huge emotional spikes and our rider can stay dormant—both of which feel comfortable inside our minds. However, life doesn't always work that way. Life often forces us to move towards the unknown. It forces us to face our fears and decide how to move forward towards the uncertainty that lies ahead. But hear me clearly, we are clingy by nature, and we will fight like hell to keep the familiar parts of the shoreline in sight. Any situation forcing us to leave our comfort zone keeps fear and anxiety coursing through us, and when fear is present, we manifest fear-based behaviors that are observable to those outside of us.

If you doubt this, simply look at most new hikers as they leave the starting terminus on their long-distance journeys. Many have 80-liter backpacks shoved so full they have to attach items to the outside of their packs. It's the only way they can carry what they "need to survive." This huge backpack, with items flailing around on the outside, gives the appearance of a modern-day gypsy pushing north towards their destination.

I don't say this to poke fun, I say it to highlight where most of us are when we try to separate from our Matrix lives and move towards uncertainty. It's analogous to letting go of the side of the pool when you tried swimming in the deep end for the first time. The wall is safe and comfortable; the deep water is scary and unknown. So, instead of simply letting go of the wall and swimming, we cling to an armful of water noodles to ensure we will be safe. In reality, we aren't really swimming in the deep end. Our elephant forces us to cling to anything that will anchor us to our familiar shoreline. My question to you is this: What are you clinging to in your life?

When an aspiring thru-hiker starts their journey, the rider sees a wealth of uncertainty on the path and tries to create practical solutions to the perceived problems ahead. However, if you have never thru-hiked before, and if you did very little preparation, the rider doesn't have much to work with as he tries to assess past experiences to make his future predictions. This uncertainty will trigger our fear response and our elephant will nudge us to keep stuffing more "survival items" into our backpacks. The elephant tells the rider to either calm my nerves with competence and confidence or plan on carrying more equipment to make me feel safe. Since the rider doesn't have the competence or confidence yet, he concedes to the elephant's solution of carrying more gear. Like Dr. Brewer's formula predicted, the anxiety created by the unknown produces the felt need for hikers to carry 40 or more pounds of kit on their backs. It's the armful of water noodles manifesting inside the hiking context. Somehow, carrying 40 pounds of gear assuages our fear and uncertainty.

Now, please don't interpret my water noodle metaphor as me saying that "We should be able to let go of all our fears at once." For most of us, that just isn't reality. Sometimes, using a stair-step approach is beneficial in getting us over our fears, but here's the secret most of us won't admit: We never really let go of the water noodles in our lives. We let our fear drive most of our decisions. We relegate our driver to finding solutions that appease the elephant instead of pushing ourselves towards discomfort and growth.

When we let our fears guide us, we cling to everything and everyone around us. We fight like hell to keep things the same. We define ourselves by the things we cling to. However, most of us didn't choose to leave the Matrix for an extended period because we wanted everything in our lives to remain the same . . . we did it to grow and change. Yet, most of us can't let go of the water noodles, so we pack our Matrix fears inside our backpacks and carry them on trail with us.

The funny thing is, most of us thought we had our hiking kit somewhat dialed in as we took our first steps on trail. Why wouldn't we? Leading up to our start date, we watched dozens of YouTube gear videos, we read countless gear posts in the WhiteBlaze forum, we slogged through all the smart-ass answers to hundreds of questions in our hiking groups on Facebook, and we spent our remaining free time roaming online and brick and mortar stores to buy only the "essential" items for our journey.

Yet, despite all the advice to avoid packing our fears, we still carried those extra pairs of socks in case something happens to our other three pairs. We packed that face moisturizer because we might get a wrinkle if we aren't moisturized before going to sleep at night. We convinced ourselves to carry that towel in case we ran across that random shower in the middle of the woods. We threw in a second battery bank just in case our current 30,000 milliamp-hour battery (that could power a small city) won't last the four days to our first town stop. We throw seven days of food inside our food bag to hike a section that will only take us four days to complete. We try to be stringent on what we are carrying, but the reality is, our natural state is one of fear and clinging to normality. It's extremely hard to let go of the things we might need and only take the things we really need.

I understand this concept of clinging because I lived it. Hell, I still live it even after 3,000 miles of hiking. I left Springer Mountain in mid-February with a backpack that weighed right at 40 pounds. It was full of my fears and my attempts to drag some of my Matrix life out to the trail with me. If you watch my AT pre-hike gear video on YouTube, you can see all the fear-based items I was including in my backpack. To be honest, I snuck a few other items in the morning I started my hike. I couldn't let go of the water noodles completely. But the question we must ask ourselves is, Why? Why do we cling so hard to the same things we tell ourselves we want to let go of? Why do we let our pack weight become a negative variable working against us on our hike?

Our clinging is tied to our fears, and our fears create anxiety. Until we can face those fears and reduce their influence over our lives, our packs (both literally and metaphorically) will continue to be stuffed with excessive crap that we don't need for our journey. It becomes this self-induced struggle of carrying too much weight on top of a body that has its own challenges without the added weight of our fears on top. Instead of helping our body climb the mountains of North Georgia, we load it down and force it to carry our heavy-ass fears.

The extra weight we are carrying will bring out the mental demons early. When the physical pain begins in earnest (and it won't take long), it will trigger our elephant's negative emotions and leave our rider with problems he can't fix. Remember, the rider is looking forward and trying to predict the problems that are on the horizon. He already tried to convince us we were packing too much crap, but our elephant's fear overruled that one. Once that decision was made, our rider accepted it and won't waste more energy considering it in the future—at least not until our elephant releases some of its fear surrounding the unneeded items. This friction creates mental chaos and leaves us at the mercy of our six-ton emotional elephant.

Instead of fixing the real problem, we blame all the external variables that surround us. We blame the mountains, the cold, the rain, the snow, the bugs, an injury, and anything else we can point to outside of ourselves. We love to pretend these items are the main causal factors. In reality, it was our fear and clinging that got the chaos party started. Think about how much easier the mountains in Georgia would be if we only filled our packs with what we need versus what we are fearful we might need. Would our lungs still feel like they are going to explode at times? Would our legs, knees, and feet still ache? Would the cold, wet rain still suck? Of course, but the severity of these ailments will be reduced significantly if we aren't suffering from the compounding effects of carrying the weight of our fears. A journey of this magnitude is about controlling what you can control so you have the energy and patience left to deal with things you can't control. Using a baseball analogy: when we let our fears dictate our actions, we step up to the plate with two strikes against us, and our margin of error is reduced significantly.

Pointing the finger back at myself for a moment, I was lucky because I keep my body primed for strenuous events like a thru-hike. Even though I carried too much weight as I stepped off at Springer, it didn't have such a negative effect on my mind and body. Don't mishear me, my body still felt wrecked by the time I made it out of Georgia, but my years in SOF and my body's ability to carry heavy loads got me through it. Eventually, after several weeks on trail, my elephant started growing more confident and less fearful of the "what ifs" that existed in front of me. Why? Because the competence gained through experience is often the key to unlock the cage of fear.

I eventually sent home items that never came out of my pack. I began purchasing lighter equipment and switched out my heavier items. I let go of my military mindset around wearing boots and moved to trail runners. Maybe most importantly, I was still cautious of the unknowns of the trail ahead, but my confidence kept me pushing towards them. Fears can't survive if we keep moving towards them, and when the fear no longer controls us, we stop clinging to normality.

This point is important for ALL aspiring long-distance hikers to realize. If you can push through the pain and fear in the early stages of your journey, the competence and confidence you are gaining will help subdue the fears of your elephant. When new hikers find ways to stay on trail long enough to gain competence and confidence, most can end the desire to cling to the items they swore were essential before they left home. For some it happens gradually, kind of like they are releasing one water noodle at a time. For others, their new confidence allows them to release all the noodles at once, as they send home all the extra junk they have been carrying. Regardless, the growth happens, and this growth is the key ingredient to a successful thru-hike.

Even more exciting, once we learn to release our fears on trail, we intuitively shift that same spotlight of awareness towards our larger life. We see things from a new perspective and can begin letting go of the Matrix side of ourselves as well. Do you want to know why hikers struggle with post-trail depression and why they long to be back out on trail? It's because they learned to let go of the fear and clinging in their lives, and the Matrix doesn't feel like home anymore. They swallowed the red pill and no longer identify with the world inside the Matrix. They no longer define themselves through the people and material items in their life. They have finally found their true self—the part of us that has always been there waiting to be discovered.

Here is the biggest point to drive home: This growth only happens to hikers that stay on trail long enough to experience it. It can be argued that 75 percent of hikers never experience this growth because their fears convince them to head back to their Matrix lives and cling to their armful of water noodles. They choose to cling to normalcy instead of continuing to push north towards their fears. Only one of those choices brings fulfillment to our lives, and it isn't normalcy.

The point to these last few paragraphs is that we will never dial in our pack weight perfectly before we gain the competence and confidence on our hike, but if we want to give ourselves the best chance to make it long enough to experience the growth, we must reduce as much weight as our elephant will tolerate. We must prime our bodies to withstand the rigors of the North Georgia mountains. We must realize that we are clinging to our fear and trying to swim against the current of life to keep the familiar parts of the shore in sight. If we can prime ourselves before we step on trail, we can gain confidence and competence much earlier in our journey.

To do this, we must be able to look at ourselves critically. It would be beneficial if you can gain some awareness of what you are clinging to in your Matrix life before you hit the trail. Reflect on your life and decode what underlying fears are driving your behavior. Be painfully honest with yourself. Figure out what you cling to and write it down. If you have a spouse or a close friend, ask them for their perspective. Give them permission to be blunt with you and be grateful to them for being honest.

What do they see you clinging to? Do you fear being alone and must always have someone around you? Or, if you are like me, do you fear being around people and cling to isolation from social interactions? Do you fear being cold or extremely uncomfortable? Of course you do, our brains are wired that way. Do you fear bears or other wild animals? Do you fear the dark? Again, of course you do. We are here today because our ancestors survived by utilizing these same fears. However, each person reading this struggles with one or two fears more than others, and this is what I want you to discover before your hike.

For me, I have been conditioned to be comfortable in the dark, hiking alone for days on end, and camping in the middle of nowhere amongst the wild animals. If we are being honest, the AT is a great trail to hike for those fearing being eaten by a bear or other wild animal. On the risk meter, it doesn't even register as a concern for me. But here is the fear that I still struggle with after 50 years on this earth and 3,000 miles of hiking. Food. Yep, one of my nagging fears that often drives my behavior is being without food. You may wonder how that can be since I spent over 20 years in SOF learning how to perform my job under harsh conditions like not eating for days. I believe it was these very experiences that led to my fear of being without food.

If you ask my wife, she can tell you about my insane habit of stocking our pantry to the gills with food. When I am hiking, you can rest assured that my food bag is much heavier than it should be. In fact, I never hiked into a town on the AT without at least two full days of food remaining in my food bag. Think about that for a moment. Two days of food for me equals around four and a half pounds (I eat a lot). Thus, my fear of being hungry led me to carry almost five extra pounds for 2,200 miles. It's the equivalent of carrying a five-pound rock the entire way. If you are one of those who just read what I admitted to you, and are telling yourself, "It's better to be safe than sorry," then I argue that YOU just identified yourself as someone that will tend to pack your fears. That's not an indictment, that's a helpful nudge. Those are the mindsets I am trying to nudge all of you to find in your own life. What are you clinging to, and what is the underlying fear causing it?

My food fear has become a fun challenge for me to try and overcome. I thru-hiked the Pinhoti Trail in 2020, and it gave me 380 miles to practice packing only what I needed. To be honest, I failed miserably, but I did better than on the AT. I then thru-hiked the short 72-mile Foothills Trail in December 2020 and did a little better, but I still have progress to make. My food fear still triggers my elephant every time I am in town buying my resupply. The next thing I know, the buggy is full enough to do a hiker feed for 20 hikers. Ugh . . . it's still a struggle for me and I will battle with it in the future for sure. However, the best part is, I'm more aware of this fear-driven tendency and can deliberately focus on it when I am doing my food bag loadout. This awareness has helped me gain confidence in how much food I really need versus how much my fear tells me I need. If we can shine our flashlight of focus and awareness on the dark corner of our fears, we can start eroding the control they have over our lives.

Diving a Little Deeper

I am going to scratch more of the paint off this conversation and take us a little deeper than some of the surface fears we have discussed so far. One of my deepest and most challenging fears is the worry for my family's safety and comfort when I am away for extended periods. Again, it's easy to deduce that my time spent overseas on multiple combat deployments was the inception point of this fear. Having to hug your wife and infant son goodbye before a combat deployment, unsure if you would ever hold them again, was rough to experience repeatedly. I consider myself luckier than most because I had many reps dealing with this separation before my AT thru-hike in 2017. However, this deep-seated fear became my biggest mental demon on trail. I could no longer use the "I have to go fight the enemy there, so they don't come here" reasoning and apply it to my absence on my thru-hike. This journey was totally voluntary and that added a mental complexity layer I wasn't ready for.

My elephant kept throwing emotional spears at me daily, reminding me I left my family at home to fend for themselves. There were many days I felt selfish and ashamed, and it was mentally challenging to fight through it and keep pushing north. But this is the point, so don't miss it: the fear I had was unfounded, and the clinging to my guilt for being gone so much in the military kept manifesting itself seven years after I had retired. This fear, and my clinging thoughts of "I should be home with my family," created some enormous mental demons for me during my hike.

All of us have our own experiences and fears that WILL find us during these long-duration journeys. Times when we are alone with our thoughts and facing some extreme physical and mental challenges. The question is, How will we handle these moments when our elephant injects these negative emotions (fear, anger, anxiety, impatience, regret, shame, self-pity, resentment, and many more) into our experience? How will we keep ourselves on the desired path and avoid being consumed with these debilitating emotions? How do we keep our purpose and meaning in focus and not let our motivation be diverted by negative thought patterns?

The truthful answer is, we don't. The negative thoughts are coming. It's how we react in those moments and keep pushing forward that makes all the difference in the world.

When the mental demons come calling, we can apply some simple and universal techniques to endure their barrage on our minds. The first and most helpful tip I can offer is to get the mind and body back into alignment. When our rider is focused on solving problems, or our elephant ruminates on past events that we don't want to repeat in the future, our minds lose synch with our bodies. Our minds either project themselves into the rider's future or the elephant's past. When this happens, our consciousness shifts with them and leaves our body to fend for itself. How do I know this is true? Here is a quick experiment you can conduct with yourself to witness this separation.

Spend one minute focused on your breathing. Breathe in slow, deep inhales through your nose, hold it for four seconds, and release this breath slowly for a count of six. Repeat this sequence for one minute. Once complete, I want you to solve the following math problems in under 30 seconds. You can use your phone's calculator if you wish, just have them completed in less than 30 seconds. Ready . . . go!

13÷27 =

143 x 255 =

12,311 ÷ 7 x 876 =

Hopefully, you completed the math problems in the time allotted. More importantly, I want to know what happened to your breathing when you were solving the problems? Were you still in control of it? Did it remain deep, slow, and conscious? Or did it become irregular, shallow, and quickly fade from your awareness? My guess is the latter.

It happens to all of us. Our rider started solving the math problems and recruited all our focus and energy towards completing the problems in under 30 seconds. We unconsciously discarded the one aspect of our biology that we can control to keep us calm and measured, and went all-in on the problems confronting us.

Our breathing is thankfully an automatic function of our body, but we can also control it when needed. In fact, it's one of the easiest ways to nudge our nervous system into a parasympathetic response (rest and digest) and out of a sympathetic response (alertness and stress from real or imagined fear). If I can become aware enough in the moments of fear, anxiety, and stress, then I can align my mind with my body—meaning bring my thoughts back to the present moment where my body is always located. By regulating our breathing with our diaphragm, we can regain our mind-body alignment and reduce the erratic breathing patterns that often accompany stress and fear. By focusing our narrow beam of attention on our breath, we can begin healing ourselves from our self-created fear and suffering.

The best way I have found to recognize when my mind-body connection is out of synch is by asking myself where my head is right now. Is it out in front of my body worrying about the mountain that is still seven miles away, or is it behind me still ruminating over the two extra miles I had to hike because I took a wrong turn on the trail? Either way, if my mind is not aligned with my body (AKA being in the present moment) then all the tools of biology that I can control are not available to me. I am not conscious enough to take control of my diaphragm and regulate my breath. I am stuck in a sympathetic stress response that is causing my body to: breathe shallower, divert blood from digestion to my outer extremities, dump cortisol and adrenaline into my system, continue to feel hyper-alert and searching the environment for more negative cues, and a host of other functions that happen automatically when I am anxious and stressed.

By asking myself where my head is right now and identifying the mind-body misalignment, I can regulate my breath using my diaphragm and kick-start my parasympathetic response system into action. This is a technique we should all be using in our lives whether inside the Matrix or on a long-distance hike. It's a simple method to bring us into the present moment and regain our awareness of what truly matters . . . being right here, right now. We will discuss some effective breathing patterns later in the book.

Another method to bring our mind and body back into alignment is by focusing on the information coming into our senses. Often, when I am outside and my mind starts racing ahead or is stuck behind me somewhere, I can snap out of it by simply absorbing the data pouring in through my senses. I can tune my hearing into the sounds of nature and bring myself back into alignment. I can feel the cool breeze hitting my exposed skin and snap out of my distracted state of mind. It never ceases to amaze me how dull my senses become during these moments of mind-body misalignment. I often wonder how I can tune out the beautiful world so effortlessly while my mind takes my awareness wherever it wants to go. This is the disease we are all suffering from. We rarely enjoy mind-body synchronization during our lives. We walk around asleep to the only thing that exists . . . the present moment.

The questions for us now become: How can I effectively snap out of my mind-body misalignment and become more present? If my mind is leading me around at will, and I am unconscious of it, how will I ever wake up enough to find synchronization with my body? The answers to these questions will be slightly different for each of us, but a simple nudge from your watch or phone can get the journey towards presence started.

I set several alarms throughout the day on my watch and phone to snap me back into the present moment. When the alarm goes off, I pause what I am doing and take in several deep breaths to reconnect my mind and body. I try to empty my mind and focus on what my senses are experiencing.

How long can we stay present each time? It lasts as long as we focus our awareness on either our senses or our breath. Our Matrix reality will eventually take back over, but by using these alarms, we can start habituating our minds to tune into the present moment more easily. I suggest you will find that after prolonged use, you'll become more in tune with the universe and less consumed inside states of mind that don't exist.

If you are someone who doesn't want to use an electronic resource to nudge you to the present moment during your hike, then stack it on top of another habit that you already do routinely. For example, every time you take a drink of water, wake up and shift your focus to the sensation of the cool water as you swallow it. Then shift your focus to your other senses and experience what is happening all around you. There are many other habits you can stack this awareness technique on top of, including every time you crest a mountaintop or cross a stream. Whatever you choose, make sure you give yourself enough time to feel the energy when the mind-body synchronization happens. It's like plugging yourself into a power outlet. It allows our energy to flow inside us without barriers or blockages. It's how we can overcome almost any mental hurdle we will experience on trail.

Fear and clinging are natural experiences in all our lives, but we don't have to let them control us. By becoming aware of the fears driving us, and the clinging that results from them, we can use our biology to help counter the negative effects of this emotion. Fear is healthy if it doesn't become a prolonged experience inside our minds. It saves us from the threats around us and helps ensure our survival. Yet, most of us can't turn off our anxious minds that focus on the perceived threats of the future or the lingering threats from the past. Neither exist, but inside our minds, they feel real. They force our bodies to react in much the same way as if the events were really happening. Hopefully, this chapter has provided you more awareness of how this is playing out in your life, and a few tools to start bringing your rider and elephant back into alignment.

Learning to let go of these fears and getting comfortable with releasing the physical items we are clinging to gets easier the longer we stay on trail. And here's the magic folks: once we get our equipment dialed in and learn how to synch our mind and body, we can shift our experience from one of fear and clinging to one of being present and enjoying each moment as it's presented to us. That is where we can finally savor the journey as we keep pushing north.

Chapter Nine
Our Behavior Becomes Our Biggest Obstacle

Normality is a paved road; it feels comfortable to walk, but no flowers grow.

Vincent Van Gogh

Our conditioned behaviors serve as some of our biggest obstacles on trail. Most assume that variables like foul weather, extreme cold, heat and humidity, dry water sources, biting bugs, or the never-ending roller coaster terrain will be the most troublesome difficulties on their journeys—but they're wrong. The most difficult obstacles we face are usually created by us in the form of our habits. The same habits that plague us inside our Matrix life will follow us out on trail unless we discover a hidden fountain of self-discipline not tapped into before. I suggest the 75 percent failure rate on the AT reflects the inability of new hikers to adapt their behaviors to meet the demands of the trail. The successful 25 percent learned to let go of habits that didn't add value to their trail life and adopted new habits that reduced friction and increased momentum. But before we go any farther, let's define a habit so we have a baseline moving forward.

Just the term "habit" probably lands differently on each of us when we hear it. When we think about habits for our discussion in this book, I am referring to all those unconscious behaviors that manifest in our daily lives with little effort, engagement, or energy from our minds. Habits, in their simplest form, are conditioned responses that we have developed to interact with the environment that surrounds us. Merriam-Webster defines a habit as, 1) a settled tendency or usual manner of behavior; 2) an acquired mode of behavior that has become nearly or completely involuntary.[16] This should sound familiar to you as it touches on two things we have discussed so far—System 1 thinking and our elephant.

Our elephant controls much of what we do. If we can become aware that our behavior is usually orchestrated by our more ancient, "I want it now" emotional brain, then we can understand why we behave so reflexively and have such a hard time adjusting our long-term behavior to match new challenges. What you do in your normal life will follow you on your journey if you don't deliberately alter it. In some cases, this may provide some benefit. My habit of not sleeping in and getting my day started early on trail paid many dividends in my ability to hike big-mile days. I don't hike 25 miles a day over mountains because I hike fast. In fact, I hike fairly slow when compared to many others. But I'm absolutely savage at getting on trail early and taking minimal breaks during the day. Why? Because it's a habit I have been nurturing my entire adult life. I am up no later than 4:00 a.m. and usually hiking no later than 5:30 a.m. on a late day. However, I also carried other habits with me on my journey that did not serve my desired goals well at all. They became huge mental obstacles for me during my hike and I still struggle with a few of them today.

When I started my thru-hike, I wanted to let go of things that caused so much anxiety inside my mind. Over-planning was the main habit that I needed to release. It's one of those habits that we try to convince ourselves is healthy, but it usually creates more friction than it relieves.

I planned excessively because I wanted to avoid the embarrassment of being underprepared for something. I wanted all contingencies to be planned in detail to avoid looking foolish in front of my peers. In the special operations world, this habit seemed to serve me well. In my life after the military, it has created tons of friction and has provided little value in helping me find the stillness and peace I long for.

So, as I set off northbound from Springer, I wanted to eliminate this habit and start living my life a little more carefree. I wanted my schedule to be more fluid and adaptable to the conditions on the trail. I didn't want to create a detailed schedule for my daily and weekly goals. I was tired of restricting myself to a schedule. It started feeling like a prison, not liberation. Once I set a plan in place, my overzealous conscientiousness forced me to meet the schedule and prevented me from adapting to opportunities as they arose.

I wanted to unfetter myself from the curse of time and learn to flow with the rhythms of the trail. I know that probably sounds a bit mystical to some of you, but don't misunderstand what I am saying. The animals in nature aren't beholden to a schedule or a concept of time. They are flowing with the natural progression of the universe and are never anxious about tomorrow or next week. That's the adaptation I wanted to embrace as well. To let go of complexity and embrace simplicity.

I think about it through a river metaphor. The river represents the journey—whatever that means in your context. For me, it represents the goal of hiking a long-distance trail like the AT. As we wade into the river and get to a place where we can no longer stand, we have one of two choices. In the first choice, which many of us choose unconsciously, we face upstream and swim against the current. We do this because we're scared to let go of our normality. We fear what may await us in the unfamiliar territory downstream and what it may mean in our lives. We fear letting go of our behaviors and our comfort zones. We fear changing who we are at the foundational level. Therefore, we swim as hard as we can to stay in place. We fight like hell to keep the familiar pieces of the shoreline in sight. This choice costs the rider an exorbitant amount of energy as he tries to keep things the same to satiate the elephant. Swimming against the current also keeps our elephant's emotions triggered. If he feels like normal is slipping away, he will resist for all he's worth.

Unfortunately, a large majority of hikers hit the trail, turn upstream, and fight like hell against the current. Their Matrix habits follow them on their journey and often serve as giant obstacles. Most are completely oblivious of this behavior-trail mismatch. It's why everything feels so hard when they start their hike. It's why so many fail to turn their dreams into reality. This is what my over-planning habit felt like to me—swimming against a never-ending current and exhausting myself to meet the scheduling habit I couldn't let go of. My elephant wanted to keep the familiar shoreline in sight.

The second choice we have as we enter the river is to take a deep breath, raise our feet off the riverbed, turn and face downstream, and simply let the flow of the experience take over. To wake up every day ready to adjust to whatever challenges will present themselves to us. To control what is controllable and adapt to the things that aren't. To be malleable like a blade of grass instead of rigid like a tree branch. After a powerful storm, there's a reason many tree limbs litter the ground, but the blades of grass are still in place as if nothing happened. They can flex in the face of challenges and adapt to what mother nature throws at them.

Letting the river take control of us can ignite some fear and apprehension for hikers like me who try to control everything. However, if we can be honest with ourselves, we are never in control of anything. We inject tons of useless anxiety into our experience, which makes us feel like we need to pull the reins of the elephant even tighter. However, all that does is create more tension between our rider and the emotional beast we are riding. Learning to let go is the choice we should all be striving for, especially on a journey like a thru-hike.

Our goal should be letting go of the habits that don't serve us and adopting new habits that remove friction and increase fulfillment. We can do this by focusing our rider on the critical moves and shrinking our goals for the elephant (so he isn't triggered by the enormity of the journey ahead).

As my journey began, I made it a goal to flow with the metaphorical river and rid myself of my over-planning habit. However, as I stepped on the AT and set my sights northward, this habit would prove too strong to overcome. I was not aware enough to disconnect from the moors fettering me to this tendency. As I tried to separate myself from this habit, I failed to disconnect all the ropes securing me to the dock of comfort and safety. My elephant maintained a lifeline back to its comfort zone of feeling everything was under control.

Instead of pushing myself outside my comfort zone, I went right back to my over-planning habit and continued holding myself accountable to the schedule I set on trail. But the question you should ask is, Why? Why could someone as disciplined as me not have the willpower to let go of such a debilitating habit? The answer, I suggest, is in the question itself—discipline.

Discipline was something I thrived at inside the SOF community. I had spent years up to this point refining my ability to hold the line on my behaviors, including things like waking up early, working out every day, reading books that increased my knowledge, eating somewhat healthy, making my bed as soon as I climbed out of it in the morning, never being late for any appointment, and ALWAYS meeting the schedule I set for myself. I'm not sure when this disciplined approach to life kicked in. I think it developed throughout my childhood and then my four years in the Marine Corps lit the fuse. Regardless, by the time I stepped onto the AT, it was a deep-seated process that happened well below my level of conscious awareness—and that's what makes changing our habits so damn hard!

To think my rider could simply set a new goal of "not being a slave to a schedule" was asinine. This is an example of how a good habit in my Matrix life didn't serve to better my experience on the AT. My rider kept aiming his rational problem-solving crosshairs on the symptoms, not the problem. It took me several months on trail to realize that over-planning was not the true source of the issue—it was just a symptom. The root cause was a habit that I seemed to try and suppress from leaking out—my need to be perfect.

Perfectionism has been a problem for much of my adult life. Being such a deep-seated habit, the elephant guarded my perfectionism 24/7, and no scrawny little rider was going to change it by making a shallow goal of "less scheduling," no matter how hard he tugged on the reins. If I didn't meet an established timeline or daily ritual, the perfectionist part of my elephant would wreak havoc in my mind for the rest of the day. There wasn't an option to miss a timeline on my schedule. It's who I had conditioned myself to be and was rooted deep inside my System 1 brain.

An Aside for Context

Before we go any farther, please don't get sucked into the "perfectionist" side of this discussion. I am only giving you an example from my life so you can transfer the concept to your life. If you suffer from perfectionism, then this probably feels comfortable to you . . . but don't let it. Remember, comfort and safety are obstacles in and of themselves. Become aware of the habits that disrupt your ability to find joy and stillness in your life and apply these concepts so you can flow with the current of the universe.

Back on Course

I often felt that planning out my future was the best tool I had to keep myself on the path of discipline. As I started hiking north on the AT, my instinct to plan every little detail kept kicking back on regardless of how many times I tried to turn it off. It's like walking in a room with a motion-sensing light switch. Regardless of whether you want the light to turn on or not, the system is rigged to ignite upon motion. My perfectionist habit made my scheduling behavior as automatic as the light switch—when I made any movement forward, it would always switch back on. For 2,200 miles, it often tortured my mind with the same old planning scripts I had been running for much of my life. I just couldn't turn the switch off for good.

My watch has always been a key player in this over-planning habit. My habit of looking at it hundreds of times a day to compute a time-distance measurement was maddening. If my time-distance calculation revealed that I was on or ahead of schedule, my brain would release a squirt of dopamine into my system, which made me feel good and increased my desire to keep meeting my planning goals. If I looked at my watch and was behind schedule, my brain would dump cortisol and adrenalin into my system, which increased my stress levels and brought a feeling of uneasiness and failure.

Hell, it's no wonder habits are so hard to change. Our bodies are hard-wired to keep them in place. Perfectionism felt damn good when I was perfect, and it felt horrible when I wasn't. This kept my brain searching for more perfectionism, not less. But this biological reality serves as a roadmap to freedom if we can open our awareness to it. If we can focus on changing our habits and do the hard work needed to make the change, then we know our biology will help keep it in place once established. That's freaking amazing!

My goal is to help all of you root out these habits that don't serve your journey. To help you build habits that will save your rider energy and keep your elephant as satiated as possible. The questions you need to ask yourself before we move any farther are these: What habits will I unconsciously drag onto my journey that will act as friction to the goals I set for myself? What feels comfortable to me in my Matrix life that will become an obstacle on my journey? How will my biology fight my desire to change a habit?

Maybe it will be your need to always be around other people. Maybe it will be your need to feel in control. Maybe it's the reluctance to get out of bed in the morning and attack your day with vigor. Maybe it's the habit of never finishing any project that becomes difficult. Or it might be a penchant for seeking comfort and avoiding suffering at all costs. Whatever you desire to change, the one commonality at the biological level is that it won't be easy. Our biology protects what has worked in the past and remains skeptical of any new behavior that is unproven in helping us survive.

We are often blind to these behaviors before our hike, but if we can open our awareness to our behaviors and habits as we step out on trail, we increase our chances of discovering these friction-causing habits before they derail our success. As neuroscientist Andrew Huberman stated on his podcast, *The Huberman Lab*, "The first step in neuroplasticity—a fancy way of saying to change something that is a habit or to learn something new—is to recognize you want to change something."[17] This recognition helps us focus on the behaviors we need to adjust and primes the systems in the brain to help with the change. It sounds so simple yet all of us are plagued with habits that don't serve our goals in life. Remember, inside our awareness and focus lies our freedom. We just have to find the drive, discipline, and courage to make the change.

Breaking the Habit of Planning Too Big

Here is a fact about habits that you may have never considered. Our big habits are just a ton of smaller habits merged together. This is similar to how our brains do all the hard computing in the background and only sends us the headlines. As an example, my over-planning habit spawned many smaller habits like creating a detailed mental schedule of how far I will hike today, planning a general outline for the next few days, checking my watch every few minutes to measure my progress, taking very few breaks during the hiking day to stay on schedule, trying to maintain a three-mile per hour pace, eating lunch on the move, and the list goes on and on. These smaller behaviors are the real signposts of my perfectionism.

This is why those big goals we make for ourselves rarely, if ever, work out the way we hope. We decide we want to lose 20 pounds, but don't realize there are a plethora of smaller habits fueling our unhealthy food intake and causing weight gain. Thinking we can simply turn off all those tiny habits at once is flawed. Our rider can only hope to coax the elephant by making minor adjustments, not massive ones. Our elephant needs to feel like it's making progress, not staring up a never-ending steep mountain with no end in sight.

Imagine you are trying to coax a stray cat into a kennel so you can take it to the vet and get it help. Would you stand a mile down the street with a giant bag of cat food and yell to the cat to come to you, or would you get as close as possible and place some small pieces of food on the ground that leads to a bigger bowl of food inside the kennel? This is exactly how we must coax our elephant. You must set bite-sized, achievable goals each day that will eventually lead to your ultimate goal.

I know this sounds like common sense, but what most fail to realize is that our unconscious habits, and our rider's incessant focus on the problems of the future, make narrowing our focus extremely challenging. Therefore, we must focus our awareness on which habits are serving us and which habits are disrupting our momentum. When we narrow our focus on what we need to change, it makes the change possible.

How do we attack big goals like hiking 2,200 miles from Georgia to Maine? We establish bite-sized goals and create habits that propel us towards those goals with as little friction as possible.

One example that the AT seared into my mind was the mileage signposts along the trail. Most of the signs helped feed the small goals my rider was learning to set for my elephant. I quickly learned not to look beyond a few days ahead when it came to my distance goals because doing so triggered the elephant—especially in those first 1,000 miles. These signs along the trail help facilitate this narrow mileage focus because they usually only report mileage within a day's walk. But one sign triggered my elephant to the point of making me ask myself the following questions: "What are you doing out here?" "You have been hiking for three weeks and have only come this far . . . is it really worth it?" This one sign undermined all the small goals I had established for the day and sent me into a mental tailspin for a few minutes.

For those who have thru-hiked the AT northbound, you know this sign well. It's the sign after you cross through the parking lot at mile marker 207 on the AT—the infamous Newfound Gap parking lot in the Smokies. As soon as you start up the trail behind the little restroom building, a mileage sign awaits each hiker. I have no recollection of what the top few mileage markers were on that sign, but the bottom one is still seared in my memory—"Katahdin Maine 1,972."

"That can't be right!" my mind started screaming. "There is no way

I still have almost 2,000 miles to go when I have been hiking nonstop for the last three weeks." My elephant was triggered and started dumping the old familiar stress cocktail of cortisol and adrenalin into my bloodstream. My heart rate increased, my pores began to open and produce sweat, my knees became a little weak, and I was frozen in place in front of that sign. My small goals of the day—hike 12 miles to a shelter and eat lunch, then hike 12 more miles to another shelter to eat dinner, do some body recovery, and go to sleep—were instantly overshadowed by that massive number staring back at me on that sign. My mind could not process 1,972 miles for some reason. Katahdin felt as distant as the moon in that moment.

So, how did I convince my elephant to keep walking up the trail and not beg someone in the parking lot for a ride into town to plan my return home? I simply took one step past that sign and reestablished my small goals for the day. I also walked up to the first tree with a white blaze on my path and placed my fist on it as a sign of gratitude. This became a ritual each time I stepped onto the trail for the first time after an extended break. I would fist-bump the first white blaze on my path as a simple reminder that I was blessed to be on this journey. It was also a way to use my biology in my favor.

When we do small things like my fist-bump-a-blaze gratitude technique, our nervous system releases the neurotransmitters dopamine and serotonin. When our system releases the chemical dopamine, it's our body's way of motivating and rewarding itself. In this case, my habit of the gratitude fist-bump released dopamine every morning as I entered the arena and oriented myself towards my daily goals. Taking a moment to experience this gratitude helped to prime the other behaviors and habits I would use each day to accomplish my small goals. Much like when you feel the pride of making it to the gym before work, or choosing a salad over a pizza, our system releases dopamine to make us feel good and desire to stay on the path towards things we value. It helps nudge our elephants onto a path of positive emotions and helps engender a more optimistic outlook.[18]

Serotonin, much like dopamine, is a chemical our nervous system releases to enhance our mood, willpower, and motivation.[19] Taking moments to reflect on what you are grateful for has proven to trigger the release of serotonin in many research studies. Therefore, when serotonin hits our system, we find it easier to focus on the positives and tune out the negatives in our environment. Instead of negative emotions being sparked by the realization that I still had 1,972 miles to go, my gratitude fist-bump narrowed my world back down to the positives in that moment and increased my motivation to push forward.

The best part of dopamine and serotonin is that they are free. They are the body's natural braking mechanism for the stress response. It's how we can use our biology in our favor. By creating small habits that tap into the natural "internal medicines" of our nervous system, we can overcome those moments our elephant gets triggered, and refocus our rider on the positives surrounding us.

That's why it's so critical to understand what habits we are bringing to the trail with us. This awareness allows us to see our behaviors and the negative effects they spawn in our daily lives. It allows us more space to shape our reactions and counter the behaviors before they trigger our elephant. It's the awareness to reach up and open that valve on your air mattress when your deep-seated habit of seeking comfort tries to convince you to stay under your covers a little longer. It feels bad at first, but the dopamine and serotonin release will inject positive emotions into your system as you meet your micro goal of getting on trail early. If you can nudge yourself to do these small behaviors enough times in a row, and if the biological rewards systems are in place, you will create new habits in no time. And once it becomes a habit, you no longer have to release the air out of your valve to force it to happen. Your elephant will do it for you.

Your elephant will switch its dependence from the comfort of your covers to the good feeling of getting on the trail early. It's a beautiful thing. Our biology will support our habit transformation if we can focus on what we wish to change and stick with the new behaviors long enough to display their value to our elephant. When behaviors become habits, they are pushed down to our System 1 elephant brain. This saves the rider energy because he no longer has to force a behavior to happen. And with that energy savings, we can now shift focus to another behavior that we need to adjust to reduce the friction in front of us. Our biology is remarkably easy to change if we know the correct steps to make it happen. Let's dive deeper to figure out how we can make these changes stick.

Chapter Ten
Our Habits and Change

Habits don't restrict freedom, they create it. The people who have the worst habits have the least amount of freedom.

James Clear

Chains of habit are too light to be felt until they are too heavy to be broken.

Warren Buffet

Now that we have a grasp of our underlying habits and how they can either help or hurt our momentum towards our goal, the question now becomes: "How can we prime ourselves to make habit change easier when we hit the trail?"

A cautionary point: if this is your first long-distance hike, trying to make a bunch of habit changes before starting your hike may be more trouble than it's worth. Why? For starters, most of us simply don't have a firm grasp on what adaptations will be required to reduce friction and increase momentum. Don't mishear me. I'm not saying you shouldn't get in shape or prime your mental hardiness before you get on trail. You should be savage about priming your body and mind for your hike. Those are global habits that will serve everyone well. Arguably, the better shape you are in as you begin your journey, the less overwhelmed you should be by the required exertion. However, trying to implement other habits you learned from other hikers on Facebook, or you have seen on YouTube vlogs, may sound good in theory, but if they don't match your value system and underlying deep-seated behavioral patterns, they will be much harder to implement and change.

The second reason to wait until the trail to change some of these habits is that our "normal" environment inside the Matrix makes it much harder for us to change anything. James Clear, author of the New York Times #1 bestseller *Atomic Habits*, found that habits are often easier to create in a new environment because you don't have all the same inferences and cues from your old environment guiding your behavior.[20]

Your buddies from work can't call you on your hike and convince you to go out drinking. There isn't a McDonald's on every corner on trail enticing you to pull in and order a burger with fries on the daily. Access to cigarettes and alcohol become much more restricted while on trail. There is no TV in your tent luring you to binge-watch three seasons of anything on Netflix (even though we have to be careful not to let our phones be the substitute). Without the old cues anchoring you to your current habits, you have a fresh canvas to paint the new you upon. This makes our long-distance hike a perfect environment for creating these new habits. Especially since it feels like our "survival" on trail may depend on our ability to adopt some of these new behaviors. Depending on which trail you are hiking, this may very well be true.

The behaviors and habits you will need to adopt will be somewhat specific to you. That doesn't mean doing research won't help, as I argue there is a wellspring of excellent information available on the interwebs. Just remember that those hikers ARE NOT YOU. Your journey will be unique in many ways. This means your stack of habits will be somewhat unique to you as well.

A prime example would be to look at your preference of getting up early or staying up late. Many hikers think they need to be early risers to set themselves up for success on their hike. I argue, there are tons of examples where this is not true at all. If you are a night owl in the Matrix, then thinking you can step out on trail and force yourself to be a lark (early riser) is probably going to be more harmful than helpful. It will add too much friction to an already hard process. It's like being a rigid tree branch instead of a supple blade of grass. The last thing you want is to rob yourself of the regenerative sleep required to adapt and grow during the hardest part of the trail—the beginning. Your decision to change a habit that you "perceive" to be helpful may end your hike well before the habit is ever adopted.

I suggest we should use some of our innate behavioral tendencies to our favor and save our energy for other important areas. So, for all you night owls out there, I would suggest waiting until you get on trail to adjust your sleep habits if this is a goal of yours. Trying to do it inside your Matrix life, as author James Clear pointed out, is probably more trouble than it's worth. When you start your hike, don't make giant sweeping changes up front. Be OK with sleeping in a bit longer to ensure you get enough restorative sleep. You may simply have to hike a little later in the day to make up for sleeping in. We see many night owls on YouTube hiking into darkness on their hikes to make their mileage goals for the day. It works beautifully for many of them. Before you employ this technique, I would suggest getting a few reps setting up your camp at night, and getting comfortable walking alone in the dark woods. I think hiking in the dark is an incredible way to experience nature on a different level. Don't be scared to try it.

Maybe the most destructive mistake people make when they start their journey is overestimating their body's ability. They see others hiking 15-mile days out of the gate and start feeling like they should be too. Hear me clearly because this is arguably the most destructive mental obstacle for all hikers early in their journeys: if you don't have a habit of fitness in your Matrix life, your body won't magically become fit when you step on trail. However, our minds are wired to compare ourselves with others, and it requires a lot of energy from our rider to suppress the elephant's desire to do what we see others doing. The point being, your habits in the Matrix will undoubtedly affect your hike, at least in the early stages. Recognizing the conflict of what you want to do versus what you can do will save your hike. Let's look at how these conflicts can undermine our experience on trail.

Habit Conflicts

Habit conflicts happen when specific behaviors undermine our overall goals. If your goal is to kiss that sign on top of Mount Katahdin (or insert your long-distance goal here) then you must average a certain number of miles each day to reach it before winter closes it off. We have all heard the phrase, "smiles before miles," but eventually, you must hike some miles to make it to your goal. When you have a habit conflict that reduces the number of miles you hike each day (e.g., take lots of long breaks, routinely get out of camp late, get stuck in town vortexes, show up to the trail out of shape, etc.) you force your rider to become hyper-focused on an unsolvable problem—making enough miles each day to get you to Katahdin before winter sets in. Your elephant will stay triggered because there is underlying friction that never subsides. If we don't identify these conflicts that erode our chances of achieving our goals, then we can't make the behavioral changes required to accomplish our hike.

Most of us have several habit conflicts that are easily identifiable if we can wake up enough to see them. A conflict I have experienced for most of my life is my desire to eat as healthy as I can to achieve peak states of physical and mental health. There are plenty of research studies supporting the notion that a healthy diet primes the body for peak performance, and I want to use any advantage I can find to keep pushing myself both mentally and physically despite my age. So, for the most part, my diet is consistent with my goals . . . except for one small habit—I love dessert. For me, dessert is not some kind of a "nice to have" part of a meal; my mind unconsciously sees it as a "must-have." This habit is instinctive, unconscious, and it's rooted deep in my System 1 brain. It is definitely an obstacle to my goal of eating healthy.

Relating it to the terms of this book, my elephant is addicted to dessert. He creates legitimate mental friction when he doesn't have something sweet after supper. Enough friction that even when my rider casts awareness on the habit, and he commits to putting his problem-solving energy towards suppressing the desire, the emotional charge my elephant creates is usually strong enough to nudge me to grab the dessert anyway. Again, I am extremely disciplined, but I'm still unable to overcome a simple habit that should be easy to change.

If we can be honest with ourselves, most of us have several habit conflicts in our lives. My question to you now is, What are your habit conflicts inside your current Matrix experience? What is undermining the larger goals you have set for yourself? Is your habit of hitting the snooze button preventing you from working out? Is a refrigerator filled with soft drinks preventing you from reducing your sugar intake or drinking more water? Is social media disrupting your goals of being more present with your friends and family? Is your phone distracting you from reading more books or typing 500 more words on the book you have been trying to write? Whatever your habit conflicts are, I am simply trying to nudge you to open your awareness and see things more clearly.

Like my dessert habit, your habits are comfortable and unconscious. The only way we can identify what behaviors are eroding our forward momentum is by shifting our focus towards them. By focusing our attention on what we desire to change, we prime our minds to adapt. If we can keep focused on the behavioral change long enough, our brains can rewire those neural pathways to make our desired behavior a reality. If we can disrupt these habit conflicts in our lives, we can decrease the friction and increase our momentum towards that far terminus. It's like taking our foot off the brake and pushing the gas. Let's dig in deeper to see how we can direct our rider and coax our elephants to make these changes happen.

Ridding Ourselves of Self-Induced Friction

Creating behavior that will increase momentum and reduce friction should be a primary focus in our life. We must quit wasting precious time with habits that stunt forward progress. However, humans are not the best at setting behavioral goals and sticking to them long enough to achieve positive results. Let's do a quick recap on what we have covered so far so we can merge it with habit creation.

Since our nervous system is wired to survive, it's more focused on what feels good and what's keeping us safe in the moment. It's our elephant at its finest. However, we are also blessed with the rider part of our brain that can look farther ahead and visualize where we should go. The rider decides when we need to change our behaviors to achieve a goal, but it's our elephant that must buy in, or the change won't happen. If we can direct our rider, coax our elephant, reduce the friction, and remove obstacles on the path in front of us, the habit change will be much easier. If we can identify and remove the behaviors that are causing friction, and create behaviors that support our forward momentum, then Katahdin won't feel like it's an unreachable goal. Those 2,200 miles will feel more like a welcomed journey of growth pulling you up the trail and less like you dragging an anchor behind you the entire way.

The Four Pillars to Better Behavior

1. Motivation for Change

We can discuss how to change behavior all day, but unless there is the genuine motivation behind making these changes, there is little hope we will stay the course. However, motivation shouldn't be hard to find for those embarking on a long-distance hike. Something is pulling you out of your comfort zone in the Matrix and leading you towards the trail. Although you know it will be one of the most difficult undertakings of your life, it doesn't deter you from donning your backpack and pushing up the trail toward your goal. So, again, our motivation should not be hard to find.

We will spend an entire chapter discussing the importance of building the "why" behind your journey. Your "why" will stand as the bulwark between you and the forces convincing you to quit and go back home. We will also discuss aiming the meaning behind your hike to something outside of yourself. Something that is bigger than you and will serve as your accountability mirror. Therein lies the key to your motivation. The meaning behind your hike IS the foundation everything else is standing upon. It's the secret to using our biological tools to our benefit. When we make strides towards accomplishing our purpose and meaning, we release the cocktail of neurochemicals and hormones like dopamine, serotonin, norepinephrine, and oxytocin. These keep our elephant feeling positive and satiated with our journey, and if our elephant is happy, we can maintain momentum without a lot of friction bogging us down. These chemicals also keep our rider focused on the tasks that lead to our goal. They help nudge him towards the solutions that work and away from the things that don't.

The type of motivation we choose to employ is important. Self-admittedly, I have spent a lot of my life using negative motivation to keep me moving towards my goals. Whether it was remembering someone's slight, proving wrong those who didn't believe in me, or proving I can outlast mother nature, I would always dig up some negative emotions that would help dump some cortisol and adrenaline (flight or fight juice) into my system to give me a boost. I admit, I used this type of motivation during my thru-hike of the AT as well. When it felt like mother nature was throwing everything at me to prevent me from moving forward, I would build up some rage inside so I could keep pushing north in the face of the horrid conditions.

I see many other hikers using the same negative motivation to power their hike as well. But here's the wake-up call folks, when we use negative emotions as fuel, there is an enormous downstream cost that our body and mind will have to pay later. When we purposely push our elephant to the negative side of the emotional spectrum, we bring on the onslaught of our sympathetic nervous system. The fight-or-flight cocktail of cortisol and adrenaline can become toxic inside our bodies when they persist longer than the short durations they were created for. It's why stress and stress-related diseases are running rampant in the world today. It's also the reason I suggest we can use our biology much more effectively to fuel our motivation.

By continually conjuring up stress stories to propel us forward, we leave our bodies and minds to deal with the accumulation of cortisol and excess adrenalin for hours, days, and weeks. Fear, anxiety, and rage are emotions that serve an important purpose, but our bodies are not built to deal with the continuous stream of these stress chemicals. It's an example of how we are unintentionally disrupting our path forward. We keep placing our body and mind under a negative load that feels right in the moment, but we forget consequences are awaiting us downstream. This negative motivation works so well that people simply turn to it as their go-to method for getting primed for a hard challenge. However, I am urging you to release this negative priming habit and switch to a more positive method that taps into your biology's positive traits.

This will allow you to experience beneficial downstream effects like growth, fulfillment, and joy. Win, win, win.

This is why I pushed the idea that you are not at the center of anything in this universe. That nothing is happening "to you." In fact, I want to push you to realize that everything is happening for you and your growth as a human. You are not in competition with the trail, the terrain, mother nature, your critics, or anything else. When we can let go of these negative-charged emotional beliefs, we can start using our biology in our favor. We can start using gratitude, curiosity, awe, and acceptance instead. We can begin using the neurochemicals that create positive states inside us.

Think of this like flipping on a light switch of positive emotions to create ideal conditions for our mind and body. When we wake up grateful that we're on trail, the cascade of dopamine and serotonin will create an internal state that feels like contentment, fulfillment, and happiness. Our positive thoughts can also release adrenalin, which serves to increase our focus and energy towards our goals. Best of all, these chemicals have little downside. Our body uses them for growth and adaptation. It's how we can positively motivate ourselves and keep biology working for us, not against us.

Fun Fact to Consider

I was listening to the Lex Fridman Podcast this morning, and he was interviewing neuroscientist Andrew Huberman. In the episode, Andrew mentioned the difference between testosterone and cortisol. Our bodies use cholesterol in our system to create both testosterone and cortisol. However, our bodies can only create one of them at any given time, and this depends largely upon our mindset. If we use positive motivation towards our task, then we produce testosterone, which is linked to effort and makes the process of what we are focusing on feel good. When we use negative motivation, our body produces cortisol, which serves to deplete testosterone and creates mental friction and a feeling of unease. Take-away: Use biology and positive motivation to fuel your momentum.[21]

2. Narrow Our Focus

When we look at everything, we see nothing clearly. The first step of focusing is to identify a small behavior that is causing you friction during your hiking day and place your awareness on it. A good place to start is the first few minutes of your waking hours. Why? Because these are the moments that prime your day. If you can't coax yourself to get up on time, or eat breakfast to prime your body with calories, or avoid doing simple warm-up movements to prime your muscles, then the compounding nature of these habit conflicts will create friction the rest of the day. When we place ourselves at a point of disadvantage, like when we can't force ourselves to get up on time, we often spend the rest of the day experiencing some level of mental friction. We feel like we are behind and can't catch up to where we are supposed to be.

For example, when we sleep in and don't meet the timeline we set for ourselves, our rider starts working rapidly to try and fix it. We start making rash decisions that further exacerbate the effects. We decide to skip breakfast and coffee and just eat something while hiking. We rush to pack up all our camp items and inadvertently leave several tent stakes and a glove behind. We don't take time to refill our water because it will be faster to get some on trail, but in our rush, we failed to realize the next reliable stream is over seven miles ahead. This list of mishaps usually increases as the day progresses . . . all because we couldn't force ourselves to get up on the timeline we established. We placed ourselves in a position of disadvantage to serve as the foundation of our day. Some people can set that aside and just flow with the experience. However, most of us allow this disruption to own our mental space as we spend the rest of the day trying to regain the advantage.

Using this scenario as an example, we will place our spotlight of focus on our specific behavior when our alarm goes off. Whatever we are doing to avoid getting up is where we must place our focus. Much like every river starts with a small trickle of water, our behaviors spawn from one or two small habits that compound into friction-causing behavior. Therefore, if we can override the source of the compounding behavior early in the process, we can prevent the cascading effects it produces. We have all stayed in bed too long at some point in our lives, and the longer we lie there, the easier it becomes to convince ourselves to keep lying there.

We want to identify the behavior for what it is and verbalize it to ourselves. For this example, when my alarm goes off, I simply say, "Open the valve" in my mind as I reach up and turn the knob on my air mattress. It's OK to be less than enthusiastic about hearing the sound of the air leaving your mattress. I think most of us can agree that it might be the most disheartening sound on trail. But I also know that lying on the cold ground will make sitting up and getting my day started feel like a better alternative than lying there not sleeping.

Another example of narrowing my focus is my habit of staying hydrated on trail. I argue that a large percentage of hikers fail to drink enough water during the day for a myriad of reasons. However, with the water availability on the AT, there is rarely a good reason to ever be dehydrated. To narrow my focus on the issue, I check my guidebook and Guthook app to review my water options for the day. I then ensure my water bottles are easily accessible while I'm hiking (you must make behaviors easy or they won't happen). Most importantly, I make filtering the water as easy as possible.

When I started my AT thru-hike as a newbie hiker, a water refill stop was an ordeal. It would take me 15 minutes just to filter 1.5 liters of water and be back on trail hiking again. I would stop three times a day, so the cost in time was 45 minutes of hiking time lost. Eventually, I grew tired of these long water stops. I also started avoiding drinking enough water because I didn't want to stop and go through the process. I convinced myself that I could just drink more when I got to camp later in the day. This was a terrible decision and finally forced me to narrow my focus on the specific behaviors I wanted to change. My focus became adopting a faster method to get my water.

Instead of having to stop, take off my backpack, pull out a bunch of filtering supplies, and squeeze water through my filter from a large bladder, I would simply fill up my bottles in the stream and screw my filter on the bottle. It required nothing more than bending down to fill up the bottles in the stream. I reduced my stop from 15 minutes down to less than one minute and gained back 43 minutes of valuable hiking time in the shorter winter days. It allowed me to add over two miles to my daily average.

However, I added one more specific behavior that I stacked on top of my water collection. Before I leave the water source, I say "drink a liter" in my head. I then chug a liter of water before I leave that source, and usually only carry a liter (or less) with me depending on how far it is to the next source. This allowed me to stay uber-hydrated and carry less water between stops. I think most people would agree that when we stay hydrated on trail, the mountains seem less steep, the miles don't seem as long, our elephant stays much calmer, and our rider remains clear-headed and decisive. Simple habits like hydration are available to all of us if we can reduce the friction and narrow our focus on the small, simple behaviors that add wind to our sails.

I know that telling myself to perform these behaviors ("Open the valve" and "Drink a liter") sounds silly, but again, 75 percent don't complete the long-distance goal they were so seemingly passionate about before they started. I argue many of those dropping off trail were unable to motivate themselves appropriately and narrow their focus on the small behaviors that would have supported their momentum. However, even though motivation and focus are the foundations of behavioral change, we need to use our biology to make them stable and enduring.

3. Reward Ourselves

Once my air mattress valve is open, or as soon as I down a liter of water at every water source, I simply offer verbal gratitude to myself for my actions. I realize this may seem a bit contrived and somewhat manipulative to some of you, but our biology (and our elephant) are simple systems to coax if we will just take these simple but effective steps. If I show genuine gratitude to myself for releasing my air valve, it may sound something like this: "Great job holding the line bro" (reflectively, I have noticed I always have a military flavor in my self-gratitude comments). When we follow a desired behavior with authentic gratitude, it releases a squirt of dopamine into our system and helps our brains identify that behavior as something we value and want to repeat. If I do this same drill enough mornings in a row, my brain will eventually turn this into a habit that doesn't require much energy to execute. It allows us to shift our spotlight of focus onto the next small behavior we want to change. It frees up our rider's energy and saves it for new and more important decisions during the hiking day.

Another example might be how we reward ourselves for pushing farther up a steep incline before we stop for a break. Many hikers come to the trail physically underprepared. This makes hiking more difficult in the beginning as they spend much of their day taking extended breaks to catch their breath and let the lactic acid flush from their legs. A sizeable portion of hikers get disheartened at their slow pace and the inability to hike more than a few miles a day. Those with proper motivation and the ability to narrow their focus can figure out the keys to increase their mileage and stay on trail. Those who keep focused on the wrong things will eventually convince themselves to quit and go home to the Matrix. The disappointing part of this is that the solution was right in front of them and very achievable, but only if we understand the art and science of creating small behavioral changes.

We often struggle up these steep inclines because our minds are not used to dealing with extreme challenges. They nudge us (or scream at us) to quit when the pain begins. Never forget, our default mental mode is to survive. Therefore, pushing ourselves to an extreme level of exertion NEVER feels comfortable. But just like when we are working out and trying to gain strength, we must push our muscles to the point of failure to spark new growth. The beautiful thing about people who exercise and push themselves regularly is that they have been conditioning their bodies and minds to experience the discomfort of exertion. They increase their performance by leaning into their failure point. That is the secret to climbing the endless chain of mountains on the AT as well.

You must become comfortable pushing yourself to the edge of your physical limitations, and then taking a few steps beyond this imaginary boundary. This helps you override your mind's ancient habit of quitting when it hurts. "Sadly, most of us give up when we've only given around 40 percent of our maximum effort…" said David Goggins, labeled as the toughest human on the planet. "Even when we feel like we've reached our absolute limit, we still have 60 percent more to give! That's the governor in action! Once you know that to be true, it's simply a matter of stretching your pain tolerance, letting go of your identity and all your self-limiting stories, so you can get to 60 percent, then 80 percent, and beyond without giving up."[22] I am not suggesting you go out and crush yourself every day on trail, but I am suggesting that to become mentally stronger, you must push yourself beyond the point your mind tells you to stop.

Here is the small behavior I focus on, enabling the ability to push farther up steep climbs. As I am proceeding up the mountain and I feel that old familiar confluence of physical exhaustion and mental friction telling me to take a break, I pick a tree, a rock, or a white blaze farther up the hill and make a pact that I will make it there before I stop. When I do this, my mind settles down because I just gave it an end point and it can quit sending me signals trying to coax me to take a break.

This is analogous to when we are lifting weights and establish a rep count of 10 before we lift the weight off the rack. It becomes our comfortable goal, and our minds are amazing at reaching that goal. However, our minds turn into whiny children when our spotter says "Gimme two more," after our 10th rep is complete. Our minds descend into chaos and that 11th rep feels like the weight on the bar just doubled. It's the same when climbing mountains on trail. If I set my goal as a tree with a white blaze farther up the climb, my mind locks onto that spot and pulls together the resources to make it there. But then the magic happens. Once I make it to the designated tree, I don't stop.

Even though I feel exhausted, I force myself to push farther. It may be one more blaze or the next switchback, but I don't let my mind dictate my standard. I continually try to prove to myself that I always have more to give . . . and I always do. The beautiful thing is, so do you. Most importantly for the topic at hand, I take a moment and give myself some self-gratitude for pushing myself beyond the limit my mind set for me.

By rewarding my ability to push beyond my self-imposed stopping point, I am establishing an internal environment centered on growth and adaptation, not safety and comfort. The result of pushing past our goals and offering ourselves congratulations triggers the release of dopamine and serotonin. As discussed many times before, this chemical cocktail makes us feel incredible in the moment (serotonin) but also makes us desire to repeat the behavior in the future (dopamine) to experience the feeling again.

Once our brain connects the behavior with the dopamine reward, it starts to crave that dopamine hit and helps us achieve those behaviors with much less friction. It clears the mental obstacles for us. It makes reaching up and releasing our air valve instinctive when our alarm goes off. It keeps us pushing past those self-imposed limits as we climb countless mountains. It's operant conditioning at its finest. It's biology working in our favor.

One last reward neurochemical that we haven't discussed yet but is available to you every day on your long-distance hike is endorphins. More commonly known as a runner's high, our bodies release endorphins during physical exertion. Endorphins help boost our mood, reduce stress, reduce pain, and leave us with a "euphoric sense of relaxed happiness."[23] I consider this the "magic creating" reward system because its effects usually hit us at the very moment we crest a mountain and bear witness to a magnificent view awaiting us at the summit. As you stand there taking in the scenery, your body is releasing these endorphins which help create that "magical" feeling we experience so intensely. If we sprinkle in some gratitude for our ability to push hard up the mountain, we create a cocktail of emotions that makes our elephant feel unstoppable and provides our rider with an extremely clear picture of where we should go next—up the trail to find more experiences that match this one.

Pro tip: It's important to note that although endorphins are available to all of us, it is a system that must be used to reap the rewards. If you are someone who stays in shape and has primed your body to release endorphins on a routine basis, you will experience them much sooner, and with more intensity, on your long-distance journey. If you are a couch potato before hitting the trail, then it will take much longer to experience the release of endorphins because your body is dealing with the shock of the physical exertion. What's the takeaway? Get in shape before your journey. Prep hard = enjoy hard!

This is why hiking is so addicting. It's our biology creating the desire to find more experiences that make us feel like we did when we took our first step northbound (or whichever direction you are hiking). Like we felt when we reached the 1,000-mile mark and couldn't comprehend how we just hiked that far. Like we felt when we sat in the same Vermont fire tower where Benton MacKaye envisioned a trail from Maine to Georgia. Like we felt when the White Mountains came into view for the first time. Like we felt at the end of each hard day when it felt good to just sit down and revel in friendly conversation and warm food. Like we felt when we were surrounded by Maine's majestic views and catching our first glimpse of Mount Katahdin.

Damn, I have chills right now. My dopamine system is triggering the desire to be back out on trail again. It's why so many of us feel the need to be back on trail after our hikes are complete. Our minds become addicted to the views, to the people, and to the lifestyle. It's important to remember that our reward systems are powerful enough to help overcome any mental hurdles on our long-distance hikes . . . and they will keep calling you back out to the trail to do it all over again.

4. Stack Habits Atop Habits

Now that we have the motivation, focus, and reward pillars working for us, it's time to add the most powerful form of building good habits—habit stacking. This isn't a new concept and all of you do this in some fashion already. We just need to increase our awareness so we can stop stacking bad habits and start stacking good ones.

Habit stacking is as simple as attaching a new habit to an existing habit. An example I use in my own life is ensuring the first thing that hits my stomach every morning is 10-12 ounces of water. To do this, I shape the path to make the desired behavior as easy as possible.

As a coffee lover, I want a cup of joe as soon as my eyes open in the morning. When my feet hit the floor, I head straight to the Keurig machine to turn it on. Sitting in front of the Keurig is the

Nalgene bottle full of water that I placed there the night before. Since it's there waiting for me, it takes no conscious effort to pick it up and chug at least half of it. I then go to the bathroom and come back and grab the Nalgene bottle again for my second intake of water before grabbing my coffee and heading to my chair to read, meditate, and write. But the point is, by stacking my desired behavior of drinking water atop an existing habit of making coffee, I just relieved my rider from having to make a decision in my sleepy state and reduced almost all friction on the path to my new habit. Ten years later, I still do this same sequence every single morning without thinking about it. Habit achieved!

I know this example sounds simplistic and easy, but habit stacking is simplistic and easy. All you have to do is aim your focus at the behaviors you want to adopt and add them to healthy behaviors that already exist. On trail, we have tons of time to stack habits on top of our existing daily behavior. As an example, I value recovery at the end of the hiking day, but I damn sure don't feel like doing it. So, as I light my canister stove and place my cup of water on the flame to boil for my dinner, I use that as my new trigger to grab my massage roller (or whatever recovery tools you use) and start running it over my legs and feet to get the blood flowing and work out the knots. It usually takes 5 to 7 minutes for the water to boil, so by stacking my recovery habit on top of my dinner habit, I am able to accomplish 5-7 minutes of muscle recovery every night on trail. Habit achieved!

Now, it's important to note that I do all this sitting inside my tent, and my pack and massage roller are sitting right beside me. This makes reaching my massage roller effortless. Remember, we must make these new behaviors as easy as possible in the beginning. Therefore, if I were to set up my tent away from the shelter, but planned to drag my cook kit over to the shelter to cook, I must grab my massage roller as well. My trigger becomes anytime I grab my cook pot, I grab my massage roller. They become inseparable in my mind. It's no different from when we grab our cook kit and instinctively grab our food bag and long-handle spoon. It takes no conscious effort to decide you need them because they are a part of the whole. In the same manner, my massage roller is one more piece of that whole for me. By stacking a behavior on top of another, I ensure I recover my legs and prime them for tomorrow's gauntlet of climbs, descents, mud bogs, and rock scrambles.

For another example of habit stacking, I will use one of the most important habits that we see new hikers struggle with the most—gear accountability. As I am watching the current class of vlogging hikers launch northbound from Springer Mountain this year, it seems they are losing pieces of equipment at a remarkable rate. Vlogging thru-hikers are a small percentage of the total number of hikers on trail, so one can only assume the other hikers are losing equipment at the same rate as well. If you want to outfit yourself with some updated equipment, go walk the section from Springer to Neel Gap in early March and you can probably piece together an entire hiking gear set-up.

But why? Why are hikers losing essential equipment (water filters, gloves, cold weather hats, shirts, etc.) when there are no easy means to replace them quickly on trail? When everything we depend on is on our back, shouldn't we try to build habits that ensure every piece of critical gear stays with us for our entire hike?

If you watched my thru-hike, then you may know where we are going here. I created a simple but effective habit stack for accountability that I dubbed the "accountability rock." In my former world of special operations, leaving behind or losing equipment is never an option for many obvious reasons. Thus, gear accountability was always a top priority for us when on a mission. Therefore, I may have had an easier time instilling the accountability habit during my hike than those without similar experiences, but this accountability rock habit, if applied daily, will ensure you never leave a piece of gear behind during your hike. How did I use habit stacking to accomplish this? I stacked a bunch of little habits on top of my already established behavior of packing up in the mornings.

Step one: As I wake up and prep everything for the day's hike, I ensure I don't have any little loose items still outside of my backpack before I leave the tent. Why? Because loose items outside of our tent increase the likelihood that we will misplace something and leave it. Especially if you are like me and pack up in the dark every morning. So, before I exit the tent, all loose items are already packed inside my pack unless they are items I will be wearing to hike (e.g., gloves, hat, fanny pack, earbuds, etc.)

Step Two: Once out of my tent, I identify a natural object (usually a big rock or a fallen tree) and establish it as my accountability object. If I stay in the shelter, then I will use the picnic table if they have one, or simply lay my sitting pad on the floor of the shelter and use it for this purpose.

Step Three: The rule becomes, whatever is not already packed inside my backpack MUST touch the accountability object if it's not in my hands. I lay my hiking poles on it after I take down my tent. I lay my gloves and hat on there if I haven't donned them yet. I lay my food bag on there after pulling out my snacks for the day. I lay my earbuds, my phone, my water filter, my fanny pack, my Smart Water bottles, my tent stuff sack, and any other loose items on the accountability rock. This way, I have everything I need to survive and thrive in one place and it is all accounted for.

Step Four: As I tear down my tent, I know I have eight stakes I need to recover out of the ground. To ensure I don't inadvertently leave one behind, once I begin pulling them up, I don't stop for any reason until all eight are in my hand. Why? Because the human mind is the ultimate distraction machine. Our attention is diverted so easily that we often try to do several tasks at once and we do none of them well. To combat this, I simply shine my "mental focus flashlight" on one step at a time. Once I start gathering my tent stakes, I don't stop until all eight are in my hand.

Step Five: After I finish packing my backpack, I move to where my tent was pitched and walk concentric circles outward, looking for any trash or stray equipment. Once I ensure I have 100 percent accountability, I reward myself with a bit of self-gratitude inside my head. Remember, dopamine helps tag these behaviors as "need to repeat" behaviors so we can turn them into habits. That's what winning looks like out on trail. It's using biology in our favor.

As we conclude this chapter, your goal is to reflect on what habits you want to change in your life and start making them happen. Start small so your biology will work for you. Starting small helps your rider and elephant stay focused on the changes you desire to make. These small habits will eventually become life-changing behaviors because they will lead you towards your bigger goals. Small behaviors + consistency + time = significant changes. You must be willing to put in the hard work for these changes. You must break free of the elephant's desire to always be warm and comfortable. There is no growth or fulfillment located in that bubble of safety. As Mark Twain nudged us earlier in the book, "Sail away from safe harbor. Catch the trade winds in your sails. Explore. Dream. Discover!"

Chapter Eleven
Sleep is Our Superpower

Tired minds don't plan well. Sleep first, plan later.

Walter Resich

Your life is a reflection of how you sleep, and how you sleep is a reflection of your life.

Dr. Rafael Pelayo

Any discussion about accomplishing a thru-hike or other long-duration events MUST include a conversation about sleep and sleep quality. I argue, a lack of quality sleep is one of the most influential reasons people make irrational decisions and end their journey far short of their intended goal. Let's be clear as we start this conversation; it's not the lack of quality sleep by itself that drives people off trail, it's the compounding effects poor sleep has on our mental processing abilities that prevents us from making better decisions.

As we have discussed so far in this book, we need to find a good balance between our rider's rational decision-making and our elephant's emotional control centers. In a perfect world, we are sleeping and eating well, exercising regularly, keeping our mind mentally sharp, preventing our emotions from being triggered negatively, and avoiding substances that interrupt any of these processes. Taking control of our health allows us to maximize our biology. But let's be honest, we all suffer from a lack of discipline within these core areas of health.

The problem with letting our discipline slide in one area is that it has detrimental effects on the other areas as well. None of them exist in a vacuum. For example, if we eat an unhealthy dinner, the inflammation it causes will have downstream effects on our sleep and performance the following day. If we let ourselves become overweight, things like sleep, inflammation, insulin resistance, and many other variables will be negatively affected. Although this chapter is about sleep, you can't have the conversation without discussing the other variables that affect the sleep you are getting . . . especially on a strenuous journey like a thru-hike.

We spend a third of our lives asleep. When I first heard this statistic, it saddened me a bit. It seems like such a waste of what little precious time we have in this body. However, it also made me more curious about what sleep really is. The more I've read and learned about sleep, the more I realized how maximizing sleep allows us to make better use of the time we're awake. If we get a good night of restorative sleep, our rider has more energy and enjoys increased control over the elephant and our primitive System 1 brain. This can prevent us from making all of those basic mistakes like quitting on a bad day or hiking more miles than our body and mind can handle. A good night's sleep won't guarantee a perfect day when we wake up, but a bad night's sleep will almost always guarantee a day filled with poor decisions and compounding negative health effects.

In scientificky language, poor sleep affects the top-down processing between our prefrontal cortex (rider) and our amygdala (elephant) in a sizeable way. So much so that neurologist, researcher, and author David Perlmutter stated: "When we get a poor night's sleep, our amygdala is up to 60 percent more active the next day. This means that we basically have a 5-year-old making our decisions for us."[24] Said differently, when we rob ourselves of sleep, our rider loses his ability to regulate our elephant which leaves us at its mercy for much of the day. This should smack all of us in the face a bit. The last thing we need on our thru-hike is to make flawed decisions that are controlled by our elephant with little top-down input from our rider. This explains why getting good sleep on trail is CRITICAL for every single one of us. Again, it's biology, not personality. Our preference of getting less sleep to get in more miles or to stay up to drink a few more beers doesn't override the biological fact that we must have a certain amount of quality sleep to perform effectively.

Therefore, we must figure out how to handle the predictable lack of sleep that will happen early in our hike. I think most long-distance hikers would agree, very few of them slept well in the first few days (or weeks in some cases) on trail. There is an abundance of reasons sleep is hard to come by in the early stages of a long hike and trying to combat all of them will be difficult. I thought I would be immune to this sleep conundrum when I started my thru-hike . . . nope.

I predicted I would be anxious when I started my northbound hike, so I decided to complete what we military folks call a PDSS (Pre-deployment Site Survey) of the area several months before my start date. I drove down to Georgia and hiked the Approach Trail, eventually camping near the Springer Mountain Shelter on the AT. I figured if I could condition myself to the area a bit, I could hopefully suppress my excitement and anxiousness when I started my thru-hike. Nope.

I was freaking pumped the day I started my thru-hike to put it mildly. How can you not be hyped when you are staring at 2,200 miles out the windshield, and you have zero miles in the rearview mirror? Hell, I'm pumped thinking about it right now. Realizing my anxiousness was going to be a barrier to getting good sleep that first night, I figured I'd better wear myself out hiking.

I hiked 17 miles to the Gooch Gap road crossing and set up my tent in a large field close to the road. I was in bed by eight o'clock that evening and settled in for a solid night's sleep. Nope. My mind was racing from all the newness and excitement of starting my journey. I can remember lying there trying to force myself to focus on my breathing and letting go of all the thoughts racing around my brain. Nope. If I got two hours of total sleep, I would be surprised. "No worries, I got this," I kept telling myself. "I have been without sleep in much worse situations than this. Hell, I went an entire week with only 45 minutes of sleep during Marine Amphibious Reconnaissance School . . . no little trail like this was going to break me."

This is the trap most of us fall into when it comes to sleep. Sure, we can fight, resist, and push through the initial effects of poor sleep for a day or two, but remember, the downstream costs are coming. Because sleep is a foundational piece of our biology, there is no "grinding through poor sleep," or "waiting until we die to sleep." Our biology will ALWAYS win, and the price of poor sleep will catch up to us. However, we are often too mentally foggy to recognize it. It seeps in like slow-rising flood waters. We start making decisions that don't serve our rider's near and far-term goals but do serve our elephant's desire for comfort and instant gratification. Often in our foggy mental state, the Matrix appears like a better option than our life on trail. This skewed perception might be the most unhealthy downstream cost of all.

Lack of sleep is our rider's kryptonite, and without him at full strength, our elephant's desires will win 100 percent of the time.

Imagine letting a 5-year-old child make most of our choices during a day of strenuous hiking and tough decisions. It's why so many quit their hike, get home, rest and recover for a day or two, and become overtaken with regret over the fact they quit. Once their rider regains the energy needed to assess the situation and see into the future, it becomes clear they could have kept moving forward on their journey. It also becomes clear they fell prey to a triggered elephant and a sleep-deprived rider. This realization often comes as self-reflective questions like: "Why couldn't I have made it one more day?" "What was so bad out there that I couldn't keep moving forward?" "How did I let a walk in the woods become such a miserable experience?" We can often trace all these questions back to the compounding effects of one thing . . . a lack of quality sleep.

I experienced this for myself. I'm an anxious type of person to begin with and sleeping in an unfamiliar environment never comes easy. I've always just dealt with it in the military but never realized the compounding effects it had on my performance. I was blind to the cost because my mind would become too mentally degraded to notice. Much like when we drink too much alcohol, it's hard to recognize how impaired our minds truly are. It's why so many drunk humans climb into the driver's seat when their brains are running at a capacity well below what is required to drive in a dynamic environment. Similarly, we put ourselves in this same degraded mental state when we fail to get quality sleep and attempt to hike 15 to 20 miles over mountains the next day. The only way to keep our rider in the game during these uber-difficult days is to figure out how to get quality sleep sooner than later. But trust me, it's often harder than one would initially think.

As I left Gooch Gap on the morning of day two, I was telling myself that tonight would be better. If I could hike another 17 to 20-mile day, I should be tired enough to pass out into a deep slumber. Nope. After an 18-mile day, I found a great campsite, ate a warm dinner, put on my comfy sleep clothes, and even took an over-the-counter sleep aid. My efforts should have been rewarded by a regenerative night of sleep . . . but it wasn't.

Day three found me feeling more run down, sorer in my legs and feet, and less motivated than the previous two days. I was struggling up the three big climbs I had for the day and a cold rain started falling later in the afternoon. My mind started descending into negativity, and my demons were already trying to make an appearance. I rolled into Blue Mountain Shelter around five o'clock and set up my tent in the rain, mainly because there was a couple in the shelter and the male was coughing and hacking up a storm. Wanting to avoid catching his sickness, I retreated to my tent and hoped that after 50 miles of hiking, my mind was ready to get some rest. Nope. It poured all night, and a cloud covered Blue Mountain, so it was very moist and uncomfortable as I tried to get some sleep. I can remember laying there for hours on end listening to the rain hitting loudly on my ZPACKs Duplex tent. If you aren't used to the sound of rain hitting dyneema fabric, it's very loud. Three nights in a row with almost no sleep.

Day four found me hiking over more steep North Georgia mountains and feeling even more rundown and achy. The compounding effects of sleep deprivation expand well beyond simple mental fogginess. Our body also suffers from the absence of the restorative sleep it needs to repair, heal, and prime itself for the next hiking day. All the minor damage we do to our muscles, ligaments, and tendons can't heal at night without sleep, and our body starts descending into its own funnel of pain and compounding injuries.

I trained for this hike for my entire adult life. Before I stepped foot on the AT, I spent 25 years working out religiously and priming my body for events like this. I kept telling myself that the increasing pain I was experiencing in my knees must be a fluke. There was no way my body was breaking down after only 60 miles of hiking. Sleep or no sleep, my body should be able to handle the simple act of walking 15-17 miles on trail without breaking down. Nope.

I would only make it 13 miles to Addis Gap on day four. My body was hurting, my mind was cloudy, and after only four days of hiking, I was perceiving the negative side of everything surrounding me. Each climb became steeper in my head, the cold wind became more frigid as it hit my exhausted body, and each step felt like a mile. I had been to this mental and physical pain cave many times in my life, but repetitive experience doesn't make it any less difficult. It sucked every single time.

To make matters worse, the closest water source was .5 miles down a steep hill. So, after an additional mile of hiking just to get my water for the evening, I was in a dangerously low mental and physical state of being. I had to figure out something soon because I knew what was coming next in my sleep-deprived state. I argue that the effects of sleep deprivation are different for everyone, but in my experience, days four through six bring the onslaught of mental demons in my head. I knew thoughts of quitting were coming in force if I didn't figure out how to get some sleep tonight.

I also knew that I would reach Dick's Creek Gap and the Top of Georgia Hostel the next day. Most would see that as a blessing; I saw it as a natural place for my mind to convince me to quit. I would nudge all aspiring long-distance hikers to be extremely wary about reaching towns on trail and how our elephants use them to convince us that safety and comfort feel much better than hiking more miles on trail. By the time we reach most towns, our bodies and minds are usually exhausted and ready for some recovery. The problem is that our riders are usually not thinking effectively, and our elephants are usually in control during these periods of degradation. Quitting comes much easier when our elephants are in the captain's seat.

As I sat there in the warm evening sun at Addis Gap, I knew my demons were coming for me the next day if I didn't find some sleep. I ate some ramen and chicken, wiped myself down with some baby wipes, and climbed inside my tent around 6:30 p.m. The next thing I remember was getting up to pee around midnight (I hadn't learned the value of a pee bottle at this point) and then sleeping straight through the next four hours until my eyes popped open around 4:00 a.m. Finally!

Yep, it finally happened. I fell asleep rapidly and enjoyed my first actual night of sleep since I had started the trail. What effect did a simple nine hours of sleep have? If you watch my "ER's AT Thru-Hike: Day 4 and 5 a.m." video on YouTube, you can hear that my rider was back in the game, and my elephant was back under control. I mentioned in the video that sleep finally came, and I felt like a new man. Sleep changed the whole game that day and luckily, I wouldn't have any more issues sleeping the rest of the time on my hike. In fact, I miss those nights on trail because after my body and mind adapted to the environment, those became the best nights of sleep I have experienced in my 50 years on this planet.

I hiked the remaining eight miles to the Top of Georgia Hostel and got to spend the day recovering, washing clothes, eating at the country buffet in town, and meeting some cool hikers staying with me in the bunkhouse. What I didn't suffer through was my elephant harassing me with thoughts of quitting. Although my knees were swollen, my feet had blisters, and I had already lost five pounds, I couldn't have been happier. Life was good, not because anything in the universe was different that day, but because I could attune to its beauty now that my mind and body had some regeneration. But here is the takeaway . . . those mental demons are eventually going to appear on a long journey like a thru-hike. Our goal is not to eliminate their appearance because they are coming whether we like it or not. Our goal should be to reduce their impact by using our biology to our favor.

Do you know how your mind and body will react when you

haven't slept well and have nothing but mountains in your path? That was the reason I shared my sleepless first few days on trail with you. Most of us don't know what awaits us when we descend into the depths of exhaustion and fatigue. Our elephants rarely allow us to get that far in the Matrix before they call knock-it-off and force us back to safety and comfort. Your elephant will do the same thing to you on your hike if you don't have a plan. So, let me ask you: What is your plan when you don't find good sleep on your hike? How will you push through the mental demons that are waiting in the shadows?

We should also gain an understanding of the process of sleep itself. If we can appreciate how our body heals itself through restorative sleep, then maybe we can nudge ourselves to get more of it.

The Basics of Sleep

It is first important to recognize that sleep theory is evolving fairly quickly in the world of research and science. When I first became interested in sleep quality to increase performance, scientists concluded that there were five stages of sleep. Now, many scientists at the leading edge of sleep research have updated the model to the four stages we will discuss next. Regardless of the number of stages, the important part here is that the underlying foundation remains the same . . . sleep is a critical piece in our lives and we must get better at using it to increase our quality of life—whether on trail or at home. Let's dig into the weeds a bit on the sleep stages and how we cycle through these stages during the night.

At its foundation, sleep has four stages—the first three are considered NREM (non-rapid eye movement), while stage four is considered REM (rapid eye movement). These four stages run in approximately 90-minute cycles (slightly different for each of us), and we hope to get in 4-6 quality cycles every night. We only spend a certain amount of time in each stage during a cycle, but we revisit each stage throughout the night. Therefore, optimal sleep isn't defined by the sheer length of time we sleep, but how much quality time we spend in the stages as we progress through them. If I'm awakened early in a cycle because I have cortisol coursing through my system due to stress, or if I have a condition like sleep apnea that interrupts my continuity of sleep, the chances of reaching the deeper restorative stages of sleep are greatly reduced.

Stages one and two are shallow levels of sleep and serve as primers for the more restorative stages three and four. Stage three is considered a deep-sleep stage and is more prevalent during the first half of the night. It is critical to our body's recovery and growth. So, even though we might not get a full night of sleep, evolution ensured stage three happened early enough to prime our bodies for physical activity the next day.

Stage four (REM) is more prevalent during the second half of the night and governs our cognitive regeneration processes, like memory, learning, and creativity. I compare this stage to running the defragment program on our computer. All the day's fragments of knowledge and experience are shuffled around and merged to enable faster processing once complete. REM is also noted to dampen the effects of difficult or traumatic experiences we had during the day before. This is why the axioms "Just sleep on it," and "Never quit on a bad day," are such excellent advice, especially if we can get some restorative sleep in between the bad events and our decision about what action to take in response. It's another example of our biology helping us gain momentum and reduce friction.[25] However, if we don't reach stage four during the night, much like I failed to do on the first few nights of my hike, then those trauma-dampening effects won't take place in our brains. This is why everything feels magnified and starts compounding on us mentally when we lack proper sleep. This will continue to escalate until we can get some quality sleep and let stage four do its magic.

On trail, if my sleep system is not dialed in and I keep getting cold, or if my body is so sore that it wakes me up every time I move, the deeper stages of sleep will be elusive. For those initial nights on trail, the excitement, anxiety, and fear will often prevent us from reaching the regenerative stages we so desperately need. Therefore, we MUST have a strategy on how to conduct business the next day so we don't compound the effects of poor sleep. Remember, we must establish contingency plans while our rider has the energy to think clearly. Waiting until we are stripped of quality sleep is a sure way for the 5-year-old to sneak into our decision matrix.

Since we are in full control of our schedule on trail, we can create a simple plan for those days after a night of crappy sleep. Several options include reducing the miles we hike, drinking more caffeine throughout the day, drinking more water and electrolytes to ensure our brains and body can function appropriately, heading into town to rest, taking more breaks throughout the day to allow for recovery, taking a nap on trail during the day, hiking around someone you enjoy and feeding off their energy, and the list goes on. We have a Chinese menu of options available to us and picking what fits us best is important. But remember, we have to plan ahead to avoid the 5-year-old from taking over our decision processes.

Now that I understand more about this subject, my basic plan after a night of poor sleep looks like the following: I still plan to do 20-25 miles, but I let go of my aspirations to hike for long periods without taking a break. I deliberately force myself to take more breaks, drink lots of water and electrolytes, eat food that isn't loaded with refined sugar, and drink several cups of coffee or tea throughout the day. I also do some mindfulness meditation while I'm walking to try and synch my mind and body. I notice that poor sleep triggers my negative emotions more easily and meditation helps to gain back some cognitive control for my rider. When I choose my campsite for the night, I avoid sleeping in shelters where I don't control the variables of snoring hikers and mice. I opt instead to sleep in my tent in a secluded area.

If you think about it, all we're doing with our strategy is reducing the obstacles on our path since we know our mental state will be degraded. It's why understanding the rider, elephant, and path are so important. If I get a good night's sleep, I know my rider will have the authority to control the elephant much more effectively. However, even on the good days, I know I must shape my path in the afternoons because my energy levels bottom out after lunch and my rider loses his grip on the elephant's reins. On the days after poor sleep, I have to shape the path from the time my eyes open to the time they close.

One more important concept to consider after a poor night's sleep is to avoid worrying about the sleep we didn't get. I am terrible with this. Before I even climb out of bed, I start telling myself how rough the day is going to be because of the crappy sleep I had last night. It's ridiculous really. I create negative expectations before I have the chance to get on trail and measure the day for myself. Some of my best and most creative days have been after a poor night's sleep. In fact, I am writing these words today after several nights of poor sleep and my thoughts and ideas are flowing well.

I am not suggesting robbing ourselves of sleep on purpose, but I am suggesting that we don't discount how beautiful our day is going to be simply because we got a poor night's sleep. Remember, we control our perceptions of the world. If we perceive heaven, we will experience heaven. The opposite is true as well. Therefore, when you start your day after getting little to no sleep, don't set expectations. Take each moment as they come and apply some of the tips in this book to make your experience enjoyable. Tend to your rider, coax your elephant, and clear some obstacles on the path in front of you. It all comes down to adapting to the conditions in the moment. That begs several questions that all of us need to answer before we step on trail.

Consistency is Key

What is your plan going to be to adapt to trail life as quickly as possible? How will you react those first few nights when sleep is elusive, your body is screaming at you to stop, and the forecast has days of heavy rain ahead? How will you try to restore the energy the rider needs to control the big-ass, 5-year-old child that wants nothing more than to go back to the safety and comfort of the Matrix?

The number one piece of advice that stretches across all sleep studies is establishing a consistent sleep schedule and sticking to it (yes, even on the weekends). Luckily for hikers, this is much easier on trail since we don't have all the same Matrix demands competing for our time and attention. Unfortunately, Matrix sleep habits often plague hikers early in their journey as they reach trail towns and resort back to Matrix time very quickly. Staying up late and drinking alcohol is the BEST way to throw our trail schedule into chaos. It's no surprise many folks run out of motivation and money early in their journeys. They are trying to mix their trail life and Matrix life together, and those two things are like trying to mix oil and water. Some make it work, 75 percent fail. Getting consistent, quality sleep at the same time each day is a sure way to reduce mental friction and increase momentum towards your goals. Try letting your Matrix habits of staying up late and drinking go for this journey. There will be plenty of time left for that when you get back home. My guess is, most of you won't identify with it anymore.

Another beneficial tip is to stop dragging the Matrix onto the trail via our cell phones. Take advantage of being unplugged from the Matrix's news media network and refrain from watching any of it on trail. I know your habit of watching the news 24/7 will be difficult to break, but just do it. Focus intently on trail life and enjoy being able to narrow your world down to what's in front of you. You will find your mind is much less cluttered and the silly things that trigger you in the Matrix just don't exist on trail . . . unless you give them a portal to find you. The calmness of mind will enable you to achieve the mind-body connection more often, and you will find sleep to be as restful as when you were a child. Agree right now . . . no news media at any time on trail. Not in your hotel room via the TV, not in a restaurant, and never on your phone. Then email me (pushingnobo@gmail.com) and tell me your story when you get finished with your hike. I can't wait to hear how you found your freedom and the effect it had on your journey.

When I hit the trail in 2017, Trump had just been inaugurated a few weeks prior. The Matrix's media networks were rife with drama and ridiculousness that was coming from all sides. The best thing about it was, I had no clue what was happening. I was plugged into none of it, and do you know what I learned? I learned it didn't matter at all. My mind was free to focus on my experience, and even though chaos was happening in the circus known as the media, it had zero effect on me and my hike. It was incredible. I slept like a newborn baby on the AT and I can't wait to get back out on another long-distance trail again soon.

Sleep quality on trail can either be your superpower or your kryptonite. Understanding how to reach those deeper levels of sleep for more cycles during the night should be a goal for all hikers. Without those deeper levels of sleep happening each night, our body and mind will start experiencing chaos. When that happens, we'll find ourselves hanging onto the elephant's reins for dear life as he runs out of control towards his comfort zone in the Matrix.

Chapter Twelve
Building the Mental Bulwarks

You have power over your mind, not outside events. Realize this, and you will find strength.

Marcus Aurelius

One of the first and most powerful mental tools we can implement before our first step on trail is developing our "why" behind our journey. I assume most of you reading this book have heard of this tool before. Developing a powerful why statement before our journey **WILL** provide a mental bulwark for us when the trail exacts its toll on our body and mind. I have never met one person—in the hiking community or my SOF world—who leaned on a meaningful why statement in times of suffering and claimed it didn't help suppress their mental chaos to some beneficial level. That doesn't mean it will outlast all the salvos from our mental demons, but it is one of the best tools we have for the battle.

I have a unique background with why statements. I, along with several other smart folks through the years, created the operator selection process for one of the most elite SOF units in the world.

I have spent the last two decades watching some of the toughest men on earth struggle with their mental demons. I've watched as their mind became their biggest obstacle during this grueling experience. Unfortunately, most of these warriors have never defined their authentic "why" behind what they do for a living. Therefore, we spend the first hour of selection nudging them to think about the "why" behind their reasons for putting themselves into the arena once again. This is to give them something to lean on when the demons come calling . . . because they always come calling.

So far, I've not had a single candidate report that their why statement didn't help them during their darkest moments inside our process. It didn't prevent all of them from quitting, but it did allow them to make a more rational decision when the time came. Our why statement ignites our System 2 rider so he can add rationality to our decision process. Without this inject of rationality, we are left at the mercy of our elephant's emotional tirade in these dark moments. Please trust me when I say that it can do the same for you.

Zach Davis tackles this exceptionally well in his book *Appalachian Trials*. A question from his book hit home as I contemplated how to tackle this chapter. Zach asked, "So, how is it that someone of their ilk (he was referencing hikers who were prior military) could cave in during what essentially amounts to a half-year vacation?" His answer: "Because, when it comes to backpacking 2,200 miles, the greatest determining factor is purpose."[26] I think Zach nailed it, but if I could add anything to his statement, I would add the word "meaning" to make it read "…the greatest determining factors are purpose and meaning." Why did I add meaning? Because when we synch the meaning behind our purpose, the intrinsic fire that we light inside ourselves will make us unstoppable.

Our meaning ties our purpose to something greater than ourselves, and this helps increase our chances of sticking with our goals.

Why? Because they are aimed at something outside of us. As an example, one reason I wanted to hike the trail was to overcome the struggles with my dominant ego. Therefore, my purpose was to spend my time confronting my ego and reduce its influence over my life. But that purpose was centered squarely on me and gave me an easy out if things got hard and suffering ensued . . . which it always will on trail. It kept my focus inside my little perception bubble where I felt everything centered on me. To combat this, I had to attach meaning to my purpose. I had to aim it at something outside of my perception bubble that was very meaningful to me.

My meaning behind my journey was the desire to become a more present husband and father, and reduce the chaos my ego projects onto my family. My family was the real reason I wanted to suppress the effects of my ego, but if I stopped short of including them in my purpose and meaning, I set myself up to make excuses to quit my hike when things went sideways. If I'm the only variable in the equation when quitting becomes a choice, it will be much easier to end my hike.

Think about it, how many competitors have you ever seen give up when they were competing for something meaningful outside of themselves? We watch humans perform seemingly impossible feats because their meaning inspires them to new levels of performance. Whether it's God, family, country, or any other variable, aiming our motivation at meaningful things outside of ourselves changes our mental landscape and creates a focus that is damn near unshakable.

When we use meaning and purpose as tools to shape our mental environment during our hike, we create a biology-supported system of reward, energy, and love to propel us forward. In his book *The Art of Impossible,* author and peak performance expert Steven Kotler explains that beneath the surface of our meaning and purpose are our drive and passion.[27] When we are driven and passionate about something, our body releases a cocktail of the neurotransmitters dopamine and epinephrine—a fancy word for adrenalin—to provide the energy and reward systems to get us moving toward our goals. But void of meaning and purpose, drive and passion are like a rudderless boat. You have the desire to move and can move, but you aren't really in control of where you end up.

We see this more than we care to admit as millions of people try fad diets and new workout plans every year. They were passionate and driven to start the new behaviors, but when it got tough—and it will always get tough—they didn't have the bulwarks of meaning and purpose to fall back on. When we don't have to answer to anyone but ourselves, it's hard to stick to any goal. Why? Because our elephants crave comfort and normalcy. However, if our purpose and meaning shift to something like: I want to lose weight so I can live long enough to walk my daughter down the aisle, or, I want to be healthy enough to play with my grandchildren when they are born, we have added a layer of meaning that is a behavior-creating machine.

Our meaning now creates friction for us if our momentum slows towards our goals. It holds us accountable to our daughter and grandchildren in our mind. If we vote to not eat better, then we are voting to abandon our daughter on her wedding day. It's casting a vote for some stranger to get the honors of walking her down the aisle in our absence. If we choose to continue a steady diet of sugar and processed foods, we vote to leave our grandchildren without a grandparent. If I voted to quit my hike, I was voting to let my ego continue to inject chaos into the lives of my family. That purpose and meaning kept me focused on getting up every morning and moving towards my goal . . . no matter what.

This is the reason that understanding our meaning and purpose is so important when things get rough on our hike. When we think about our meaning during our journey, our system adds the fast-acting hormone oxytocin into the cocktail of dopamine and epinephrine. When these three chemicals combine, we feel as if we can conquer the world. They provide us with focus, energy, and the motivation to move towards our goals. No matter what challenges we face, we will keep pushing forward. Our purpose and meaning serve as the rudder that allows us to move toward the goals we establish. They also act as the buffer when things get stressful, and it feels like the world is coming down on us. If we can learn to use our biology in our favor, we reduce mental friction and increase our chances of success.

Building our purpose and meaning can prevent those moments we convince ourselves that it's OK to stop short of our goal. Many convince themselves at some point short of Katahdin that they found whatever they were looking for and choose to end their journey. Let me be the bad guy here and say that I think this "I found what I was looking for" reason is just another excuse people use when things get difficult, and they can't find the motivation to keep taking the next step. I know that sounds harsh, but our minds don't play fair . . . they play to win.

Our elephant will use all its ancient tools to convince us to go back home and plug back into the Matrix. In all honesty and compassion, I concede that some of these hikers may have found "something" they were looking for. However, what I can guarantee is that every one of them missed out on the magic that was waiting in those miles that they chose not to hike. I can also promise that all the hikers who made it to the end and are reading this now are probably shaking their heads in agreement with that last sentence.

The ultimate magic is not found where you might expect it. It's not found in the pain, suffering, and growth that happens earlier in your hike, even though these are requirements to experience the magic when it's time. There are no set mileage markers that predict when a hiker will start experiencing these soul-enriching moments. But what I can guarantee is that it will happen . . . but only if you stay committed until the end.

If we use a northbound AT thru-hike as an example, all those miles in the first three-quarters of the trail are simply priming you for what awaits in the last quarter. I'm not talking about the expansive views in New Hampshire and Maine, the incredible towns you will get to visit, or even the momentous ending awaiting you on top of Katahdin—even though all these are reasons to continue for sure. I'm talking about the exponential growth that happens in your soul now that you have become extremely competent at moving forward.

By the time you reach the northeast, most hikers have become so experienced at the skills needed to achieve forward movement that your mind is now free to process your journey in a more advanced way. You have become an expert at the skill of hiking, and this frees your rider and elephant from the normal worries of surviving. Your rider can start contemplating the bigger and more meaningful problems that haven't been accessible in your Matrix life. Why? Because we fill our every waking hour with so much static and noise that our riders are consumed with putting out fires, and our elephants are addicted to the drama that surrounds us.

That's why it takes so long to prime our mental environment. It's hard to unplug from our Matrix lives and flush it out of our system. Most give up trying and head back home to plug themselves back in. Those who succeed were able to disconnect long enough to figure out that it's so much better unplugged. They enter a different mental state that is ripe for growth and fulfillment. I'm not saying there won't be hard days or that everything will turn into unicorns and rainbows. My hardest days were in New Hampshire and Maine. But instead of focusing on Matrix-type nonsense when the difficulty hit, my mind became highly attuned to the experience and environment. It was a mental state that I posit very few humans can find inside the Matrix. It's why I meditate every morning. It helps me reenter this mental state and stay unplugged from the nonsense happening around me.

Therefore, to tie it all together, developing your why statement is your first vote in defining your purpose and meaning behind your hike. It's the statement you will lean on when everything feels like it's coming down on you. It's the power that led the philosopher Nietzsche to prescribe, "He who has a why can bear almost any how." Your why statement is the bulwark that will protect you from the elephant's stampede when it unleashes its emotional barrage during the tough moments on trail. It's the barricade that will protect you from the rider's penchant for seeing only the negative problems surrounding you.

At the end of the last few operator selections at my work, I have chosen four candidates to be on a podcast I host to discuss their experience. My favorite question to ask is always, "What was your darkest moment during selection and how did you get through it?" I think it would be a valuable question to answer for this book as well. So, I will ask myself this same question but in a thru-hiking context. "Early Riser, what was your darkest moment on trail and how did you overcome it?"

My darkest moment by far, and the moment I was close to quitting my hike, was when my wife dropped me off by the bridge at the Pennsylvania - New Jersey border. My wife, son, our two dogs, and one of my son's friends were heading back home and it felt like my heart was breaking in two. I was in my happy place when they were visiting, and watching my wife pull away was terrible. My heart was breaking more and more with every step I took northward across that bridge. It was like I was abandoning my family and leaving them with that long drive back to North Carolina. I felt I was leaving them with all the items at home that I should be helping with. It was a dark mental funnel I fell into that day. It was a mental hell like none I had experienced in my life. Therefore, when I see others struggling mentally on trail . . . I get it. They may have different reasons, but suffering is suffering.

How did I overcome it? Well, the obvious answer would be because I had a strong meaning and purpose propping me up during the hard times. For the most part, that is true. However, you must understand that when the demons come calling, your elephant is going to unload its emotional barrage on you in ways you can't imagine. The solution is never as simple as pulling out your why statement and reading it to yourself. There may be some instances where that will be enough, but not for the truly dark days on trail. Those require the ability to withstand the elephant's emotional barrage and somehow keep moving forward. To find the grit to keep taking the next step up the trail, and then the next one after that.

That was the solution I found that gloomy spring day in New Jersey. It's the solution I offer to every single person I see struggling with their mental demons. No matter what is happening in your life, or how it feels like the world is collapsing around you, just keep moving forward. Why does this work? Because time heals all wounds and the longer you keep moving up the trail the less potent your elephant's attack will become. Once you regain some clarity of mind, you can bring out your why statement and reaffirm why you are out there in the first place. It took a good part of the day for my mental bubbles to level again . . . but they did, and yours will too.

You can watch this day play out in my Day 66 video on YouTube. I spent a large portion of the video discussing the struggle I was facing in my mind. I rarely let those emotions show in my vlogs, so you know it had to be bad for me to share it as freely as I did. You can also imagine how much I held back in revealing the true depth of the mental hell that day. Being vulnerable is difficult for most people, and I was just learning its value back in 2017. Make sure to read the comments under the video from my subscribers. They display how beautiful the hiking community really is. It's a community of love, gratefulness, and compassion. It's a community that embraces a hiker's vulnerability and helps them grow as a human.

Crafting the "Why" Behind it All

So, how do we develop our "why" statement? Start by listing your answers to these three questions. Don't worry about making them sound perfect. Just get your feelings down on paper so you can see them.

1. I am hiking this trail because ______________?

2. Completing this trail will help ______________?

3. Quitting is not an option because ______________?

My answers to these in 2017 would have looked like this:

1. I am hiking the trail because I need to face off with my ego. I need to stop letting it control so much of my life.

2. Completing this trail will help me become a better husband, father, and human being.

3. Quitting is not an option because my relationship with my family and the world around me are dependent upon me reducing the influence of my ego. The longer I stay on trail, the more opportunity I will have to work on this. Anything short of Katahdin means I didn't give my maximum effort to make these changes. Anything short of Katahdin and I will feel I let my family down.

As you reflect on my answers, notice that my overarching goals are both internal and external. Again, aiming your meaning at something outside of yourself will be a critical move to ensure you have an accountability target that your elephant can't easily coerce. If I just want to change for myself, then my elephant gets a larger vote in my actions. The elephant controls our excuse matrix and can do so without triggering our rider to get involved. When this happens, we make emotional decisions with no rational input. But when we aim our meaning to something outside of ourselves, we trigger the rider to get involved when the elephant makes his irrational pleas to get off trail.

Once you have answered the three questions for yourself, begin crafting your final "why" statement. It should be something short enough to allow you to recite it without having to pull out a piece of paper. Remember, reduce the obstacles on the path by decreasing friction. Memorizing your "why" statement is a great way to reduce friction when you need to lean on your meaning and purpose. It's amazing how lazy we can be when mental chaos ensues. The act of digging out our written "why" statement will often become a task our elephant rebels against, so make it easy and sear it into your memory. My why statement in 2017 went like this:

This journey is my opportunity to reduce my destructive ego and become a better husband and father for my family. The only path that leads home is over the top of Katahdin.

That last sentence became my tagline that I would repeat to myself when the mental chaos would start knocking at my mind's door. It affirmed to my elephant that you can whine and bitch all you want, but the only path back home is by completing this hike.

Our why statement focuses our rider and clarifies his role BEFORE we step on trail. It gives your rider the overarching theme that will guide his problem-solving as you move forward toward your long-distance goal. Many vlogging thru-hikers do this by aiming their meaning at a charity personal to them. They make this public on their YouTube channel because it's an effective accountability partner. It's hard to hang up the towel when you know that quitting means you're no longer garnering funds for the charity you committed to. Our meaning serves as our north star. It provides a narrowed focus for your rider and helps orient your elephant's emotions towards a cause that has meaning beyond your perception bubble.

My charity was St. Jude's because I'm passionate about helping children. Once my channel started making some decent revenue from people watching my videos, I dedicated 100 percent to St. Jude's. This, on top of my other reasons mentioned earlier, kept me focused on not only finishing the trail, but also putting out as many videos as possible to make as much money as we could before the hike was over. Again . . . aim your meaning at something bigger than just you. It may be the most valuable secret hiding in the pages of this book.

Chapter Thirteen
The Power of Gratitude

The struggle ends when gratitude begins.

Neale Donald Walsch

"Stop messing around and just focus!" Are there any of us that haven't heard this phrase before? For me, it became apparent I had a focusing problem when I was in grade school. I can remember getting spring fever so bad that I would stare out the window of our classroom, unable to focus on whatever painful lesson the teacher was covering. I wanted to be anywhere but where I was in those moments. My mind projected me to my yard after school, where I was free to enjoy the long-awaited spring afternoon, doing whatever I felt like doing. I wanted to feel the warm breeze on my skin and let the sun purge all the residue left inside me from the fading winter. My mind could not focus on the here and now. It was a master of missing the proverbial forest for the trees. I couldn't simply sit somewhere and enjoy the moment the way it was unfolding. I was constantly thinking about how I must suffer through my current reality to make it to some perfect moment in the future . . . that honestly never arrived. But that didn't stop me from doing it. It only seemed to make me chase it more.

If we can be honest with ourselves, we are all plagued with this diseased way of thinking to some degree. It's keeping your focus projected on an imagined future that may never manifest. It's the "If I can just make it to Friday then everything will be better" voice that starts first thing Monday morning . . . every Monday morning. It's the "I can't wait until I have more money," or the "I can't wait until I retire so I can finally be free" script that runs in most of our heads during our adult years.

These scripts are so ingrained inside our brains that we have little restraint over them as they run out of control. They widen our focus out to the point where nothing seems clear anymore. Instead of focusing on the environment surrounding us, our minds are usually somewhere in the future or past. Our mind and body are rarely in synch or fully present in the here and now. This is why we experience so much anxiety, fear, stress, and discontentment with this life we are living. It's often just a simple lack of focus on the right here, right now.

If we can learn to focus our awareness on the present moment, we can change the game completely. In his book *This is Water*, author David Foster Wallace captured this challenge well when he wrote, "Learning how to think really means learning how to exercise some control over how and what you think. It means being conscious and aware enough to choose what you pay attention to and to choose how you construct meaning from the experience."[28] In other words, we have the means of control, but very few of us know how to employ it.

When is your mind the clearest and most present? When asked this question, many of us report our minds are only clear when we are conducting some sort of physical exercise, whether that is hiking or doing some other sort of strenuous workout. If I am being honest, I get a bit disheartened when I hear these answers. Why? Not because people found a way to let go of the distracting chaos in their minds . . . that is a win for sure. I feel disheartened because what we are really admitting is we have almost zero ability to control our thoughts. That we can only gain freedom by pushing ourselves to some level of exhaustion, and it's only during these drained states that people can suppress their rider and elephant enough to experience the present moment. The question I ask after someone gives this answer is, "What are you going to do the 99.9 percent of your day when you can't hike up mountains or run to silence the chaos?" We must find ways to tap into the here and now without relying solely on physical exertion. We must find ways to silence the chaos whenever there is chaos. We must learn to "Stop messing around and just focus!"

What I quickly realized on my journey towards Katahdin was that the time I spent hiking wasn't much of a problem for me mentally. In fact, those were the times my mind was the clearest, for many of the same reasons mentioned above. The most difficult mental moments were the periods when I wasn't hiking. When I was taking a break or sitting around camp in the evenings reflecting on how ridiculously far I still had to go. Maybe most destructive to my mental landscape was my stay in towns during my journey. Those non-hiking times are when the rider is consumed with the "what's next" calculations and the elephant feels the uncertainty of the rider's predicted future.

How can we be content in the here and now when the rider sees three days of frigid weather on the horizon? How can our elephants relax when we know we are about to enter the White Mountains—one of the most difficult sections on the trail? How can I find the stillness to sit and enjoy the view from this mountaintop when I know there are still four more mountains to climb before I can stop for the day? These are the moments we need to narrow our focus and avoid being consumed by the scripts of our rider and elephant. These are the moments we need to use our biology to our favor.

Our brains release two important neurotransmitters that are at the center of our ability to plan for the future (rider) and find contentment in the present moment (elephant). Dopamine is released in our system as a reward mechanism that keeps us pushing towards our goals. If you are addicted to cocaine, dopamine keeps your mind focused on the next high and determining how to get more of this feeling. Less destructively, dopamine keeps a hiker wanting to move forward to get that next view or hike another 25-mile day because it felt fantastic to hike that far yesterday. Why did it feel good? Dopamine, that's why.

Dopamine drives us to seek more pleasure, but it can't provide the actual pleasure itself.[29] All dopamine can do is make you want more, and it will hijack your focus and awareness to get it. It feels more like anxiousness than contentment. It could be argued that dopamine is the tool of both the rider and the elephant, but its danger lies in the anxiety and "never satisfied" feeling it leaves in our minds. If you have ever seen someone obsessed with working hard and consumed with the grind of achieving more and more success, you were probably watching dopamine in full force. The problem with this achievement-focused dopamine behavior is not that a person is hyper-focused on moving towards goals, but that the dopamine response becomes so addictive, they can't stop to enjoy the fruits of their success. Their dopamine keeps them moving forward to find more, just like the cocaine addict.

We see this displayed on these long-distance trails as well. I'm as guilty as anyone. The desire to hike long hours without breaks, talking myself out of taking those side-trails to views, and chasing the feeling of making big miles each day . . . yep, that's dopamine in action. However, when we get to camp, the feeling we were chasing isn't waiting for us. If we let our scripts run as normal, our rider shifts his attention to the future once again. He's not worried about being present in the moment and enjoying our accomplishment . . . he chases more dopamine. He hijacks our focus and starts looking ahead to tomorrow's terrain and weather forecast. How many miles can we do tomorrow? Can I make it all the way into town? These are the items that bring the release of dopamine, and our rider wants more of it. Each hiker has different values and goals, that's why we say that personality doesn't scale. But all of us chase dopamine at the level of biology. This simply means we can employ tools that can help EVERYONE because the root cause is at the level of biology. So, instead of me trying to pass on some worn-out phrases like, "smiles before miles," or, "stop and smell the roses," I want to provide some tools that work for all of us if we are willing to use them.

Dopamine is the chemical that has helped humans achieve some incredible achievements throughout history, but never has it allowed those humans to stop and enjoy their accomplishments. That's not its job inside our brain. It keeps us striving to acquire and achieve more. To get that feeling one more time. But here's the secret most don't realize: dopamine keeps us focused on what we don't have and couldn't care less about what we do have. Although that feels kind of dirty to realize, we should be in awe of dopamine's ability to drive our behavior. It's truly a biological miracle in action. However, if we let it run out of control, our rider will stay locked into making future predictions and our elephant will pump a continuous stream of anxiety into our systems. But there is another chemical our brain uses to help counter dopamine's drive to keep moving forward—serotonin.

Serotonin allows us to stop and soak in the here and now. It helps to regulate our moods and feel more focused, emotionally stable, happier, and calmer.[30] It helps us focus on the things we have in the moment, not on the things we don't have. In a hiking context, it lets us enjoy that mountaintop view we struggled so hard to reach. It helps counter our dopamine's desire to move towards more pleasure because serotonin helps us find pleasure in the right here, right now. Serotonin allows us to bathe in the accomplishment of hiking that 25-mile day as we sit in camp sipping hot tea and eating our warm ramen with chicken. If we can learn to use it consciously, then we can disrupt the rider's ceaseless focus on the future and allow our elephant to soak in the joy and fulfillment of the present moment.

This isn't easy in the fast-paced, social media-fueled, excitement-seeking world that surrounds us. The designers of the most common social media platforms are not targeting your personality with their coding, they're targeting your biology through its dopamine response. These apps are designed to trigger the release of dopamine so you will have the urge to keep clicking and swiping. They fill your feed with more of the things you like and less of the things you don't. It's why I open TikTok intending to spend five minutes on it but then realize 30 minutes later that I still have this enormous urge to keep swiping to the next video clip. Serotonin is a much-needed counter to our dopamine-filled Matrix experience. We just need to learn how to inject more of serotonin's goodness into our lives.

If we gain an understanding of how these chemicals work and learn ways to ensure one chemical doesn't get too much time in the captain's seat, then we can steer our behavior towards achieving our long-distance hiking goals without sacrificing the present moment and enjoying the journey to its fullest.

Perhaps much of the post-trail depression hikers experience is created by the time they spent on trail chasing that dopamine high. Some hikers spend upwards of six months being led forward by their dopamine system. But what happens when we reach the far terminus and our dopamine system no longer has a goal to nudge us towards? What happens when we didn't learn to balance our dopamine with a serotonin response? What happens when you go home and fall right back into your Matrix slump of seeking safety and comfort? You went from being hyper-focused on pushing through fear and uncertainty to move towards your goal, to sitting at home wondering what you should do today. Your biology can't shift that fast. It would be like driving 70 mph down the highway and slamming your transmission into park. When we don't teach our systems how to find joy and contentment in the present moment, dopamine will become our master, and mental suffering will ensue.

How can we create a better balance between these two chemicals in our system on trail? I submit we should focus on adding things into our day that will trigger the release of serotonin. Why is this the right strategy? Because, for most of us, our dopamine pathways are already functioning at a pace well ahead of our "here and now" system. Our Matrix world has primed our dopamine system to function at a high level. Therefore, we need to focus on things that will reduce our rider's narrow focus on the future and help trigger the positive emotions of our elephant. We are not trying to eradicate ourselves from our rider's focus on the future, we just need to find a better balance between the future and the present. Without this balance, we will experience suffering and rarely understand why.

One of the easiest ways we can do this is through the simple use of gratitude while on our hike. Admittedly, I started doing this early during my hike but didn't realize the benefits I was gaining other than the positive vibes it injected into my day. Being grateful for the things we are experiencing is a powerful way to get serotonin released inside our brains. (Note: gratitude also releases dopamine, which is perfect because it makes us want to use gratitude again in the future to get more dopamine.) Once this serotonin hits our circuitry, it enhances our mood, our willpower, and our motivation.[31] The point I need you to grasp here is that when you create moments of gratitude in your experience, you activate certain neural pathways in your brain that, when strengthened through use, can help your brain learn to recognize the positive experiences in your life with much less effort.

Remember, our brains are focused to see mostly negative cues to protect us from danger. Many of us never counter this negative orientation of the world and live in a constant state of negativity that feels normal. Unfortunately, living in that negative state keeps fear and anxiety flowing through us with ease. Those neural pathways have been developed our entire lives and are wired strong. It's why we must spend focused energy to inject gratitude into our lives but experience our negative perceptions with no effort whatsoever. We are attuned to seeing the threats and must create a balance by teaching our brains to also see the good. If we can learn to wire these gratitude circuits together through dedicated use, we can steer our brains towards the beauty that surrounds us in the here and now.

I won't go much deeper into the neuroscience of creating new pathways in our brains, but just realize that the more you do something (think learning to ride a bike for the first time) the stronger the pathways that create those new behaviors become. It's that feeling you had when you balanced on your bike for the first time in your youth. Your brain finally wired the right circuits together to allow you to balance and pedal at the same time. The more you rode, the stronger those pathways became. So much so that after many years of not riding a bike, you could still get on it and ride it with ease. It's because you used those same pathways so frequently, they became deep ravines of habit. (To see a cool example of this learning and wiring, watch the video "The Backwards Brain Bicycle" on YouTube.)

This is the same reason negative cues come into our consciousness so easily. We have used those pathways since birth. We can counter these by wiring up our gratitude circuitry and building it up through use. In doing so, we give ourselves the gift of serotonin and embracing the here and now. So, the question now becomes: How do we integrate gratitude into our hiking experience?

Well, if you are anything like me, you wouldn't think you would have to strategize on how to inject gratitude into an activity that takes place in nature. How could "gratitude" not be a fundamental part of walking in the mountains for days on end? As we have discussed already, our Matrix mind is not conditioned to latch on to the here and now. It's conditioned for chaos. The beauty that surrounds us on trail is often overshadowed by our elephant brain latching onto things from the past or negative perceptions from our hiking experience (e.g., the biting cold wind, the pain in my feet, the burning in my lungs after a hard climb, the ache in my shoulders from my pack, the incessant gnats swarming my face, etc.). Simultaneously, our rider is focused on trying to find certainty in an uncertain future. To find the best answer to a question that has no "best" answer. These rider and elephant habits are deeply ingrained into our circuitry and leave little time for finding the good pieces inside the present moment.

Therefore, to integrate a gratitude habit into our daily experience, we need to set a few small gratitude goals for ourselves throughout the day. This will allow us to start wiring some positive circuitry together. We should open our awareness to the natural beauty that surrounds us and soak it into our souls. We must stop and absorb the glorious mountain views after a long climb, the trees that are somehow growing on top of large pieces of granite, the chipmunks that scurry into their log homes when they see us coming, the cool rain as it hits our exposed skin, the smell of a campfire as we hike past a family enjoying a weekend in the woods, and the sounds of the birds singing their mating songs as spring unfolds around us.

Integrating gratitude into our hiking day is as easy as establishing a simple routine and doing it repetitively (like riding the bike). When your eyes open and you sit up in your tent or hammock for the first time in the morning, simply think "I am lucky to be right here, right now." I tell myself the phrase, "I get to do this today," instead of, "I have to do this today." The universe has placed us in this exact place, at this exact moment. We are EXACTLY where we are supposed to be. Give thanks to the universe for giving us another day to experience the beauty that surrounds us. Man, I seriously just got chills and a swig of serotonin as I typed that.

I also use my first sip of coffee as a portal into the present moment. I focus my awareness on my titanium mug as it touches my lips. I feel the heat of the coffee as it approaches my skin. I savor the taste as it passes over my tongue. I try to describe the notes of the flavors it leaves behind (even though it's instant coffee, this technique is fabulous to nudge ourselves into the present moment). I take a bite of whatever I am eating for breakfast and do the same drill. I then offer gratitude to myself for having the tenacity to have made it to this moment in time. To be positioned at this point on the trail. To have carried these supplies for many miles just so I could experience this early morning moment in my tent. I then shift my gratitude back home to my family and thank them in my mind for their love and understanding. I then broaden my gratitude out to the universe once again, and simply say "Thank you." "Thank you for unfolding this experience in this most perfect manner."

This sequence takes less than one minute. In less than one minute, I have enabled the release of serotonin and dopamine by the simple use of gratitude. I have established a foundation of peace, joy, and harmony that the rest of my hiking day will rest upon. Amazingly, I garnered the same twinges of serotonin from writing this paragraph. Our biology is truly remarkable.

As my hiking day gets underway, I find the first blaze on trail and rest my closed fist on it for a few seconds. I close my eyes, attune my senses to the forest around me, and offer gratitude for this trail, this opportunity, and the experience that will come today. This helps release those "feel good" chemicals and centers me on the here and now. I know my focus will waiver hundreds of times throughout the day, but in the moments when I realize my mind has gone chaotic, I find the next blaze and repeat the process. It allows me to use my biology to counter my ego's never-ending scripts running in my head. It brings me back to the right here, right now.

As I reach the many views and other interesting features during my hiking day, I will take a deliberate pause at each one, allow my heart rate to come down from the exertion, and attune my senses into the scene surrounding me. I will then become purposely curious about the aspects of what my senses are taking in. I often pretend I have just landed on this planet and I am seeing these objects in front of me for the first time. Suddenly, everything around me takes on new meaning. It allows me to rekindle the wonder I had as a child when I experienced things for the first time and questioned how they worked. A waterfall, a giant tree, a bug, a warm breeze . . . all of it.

My curiosity brings me into the here and now and ignites gratitude and awe on a grand scale. Again, this takes less than a minute at each view, waterfall, pasture, etc. Most importantly, it counters the obsessive drive to keep pressing forward and chasing the dopamine release that is waiting for us up the trail. Creating a deliberate gratitude schedule during each hiking day can increase your ability to squeeze maximum joy and fulfillment out of your time on trail. It can also prevent you from becoming a puppet to the dopamine master calling you from just around the next bend. Our dopamine master is always "just around the next bend." It takes serotonin to ease the urge to move forward and enjoy the here and now.

If we can turn gratitude into a daily habit in our lives, then many of us can avoid suffering from post-trail depression. It's the deliberate integration of serotonin into our lives, the ability to focus on what we have in the here and now, and learning to let go of what we feel we are missing. If we can use our biology to increase our joy and contentment, we enable ourselves to play different cards during each situation that arises. When we fail to use our biology in our favor, we fall prey to the conditioned mind that will create anxiety, fear, and suffering on a routine basis. We will never learn to enjoy the perfection that is unfolding in front of us.

I will end this chapter with a quote that I feel sums up the power of gratitude on our hikes and in our lives:

> *Gratitude is one of the strongest and most transformative states of being. It shifts your perspective from lack to abundance and allows you to focus on the good in your life, which, in turn, pulls more goodness into your reality.*
>
> Jen Sincero

Chapter Fourteen
The Alter Ego Effect

An alter ego is a model for how you would like to show up in some context of your life. It's going to help you succeed in the way you most want to.

Todd Herman

This chapter is meant to be both fun and useful in ways you haven't considered since you were young. We will tap into some tools you perfected as a child but probably haven't used since. What we once considered a secluded world of play and fantasy held some amazing lessons in overcoming the obstacles in our path.

As children, we rarely played as ourselves. What fun would that be? Instead, we imagined we were a character that we admired from television or the movies and sourced their talents in our world of imagination. Whether conquering imagined foes in a far-off galaxy or using a character's bravery to overcome our personal fears in a real-life situation, taking on the identity of an alter ego seems to be coded somewhere inside our genes. It's an innate technique children use to overcome their fears or muster the courage to act in ways that don't come naturally to them. It's not that they don't possess these traits, it's that they have a hard time bringing them to the surface when needed. By using an alter ego, they simply unleash their desired behavior much more easily. What I'm pushing you to consider is that you can tap into these same techniques to overcome the obstacles on your journey as well. Using an alter ego is a great way to overcome life's obstacles when you can't muster the desired behavior with the "normal" you.

"Early Riser, what in the hell are you talking about? Are you saying you want me to play pretend while I am on my thru-hike?" Well . . . yes. Let me explain the concept a little deeper. When you were young, I guarantee there were times you had to do something you perceived as scary and difficult. Something that called on behaviors or talents that didn't fall inside your comfort zone of normality. One way we overcame many of these challenges was to turn ourselves into someone else. For me, I can remember pretending I was characters like Rambo or Luke Skywalker (yes, I grew up in the late 1970s and early 1980s). I wouldn't run around all day pretending I was them; I only called on them when something fell outside of my comfort zone and I needed to draw on their qualities that didn't come naturally to me. I saw Rambo and Luke as figures with the strength and courage to stand for what they believed in and who wouldn't back down under threat. They had the grit to push towards their goals despite their fear.

We all have a trapped self inside us. To help us understand this better, let me ask you a question: Who is the alter ego when we think of Superman? Is it Superman or Clark Kent? If you said Superman, well . . . your System 1 brain got you again. Clark Kent is Superman's alter ego. He is a character that allows Superman to interact effectively inside the Matrix and not be discovered. It allows him to be in a better position to keep tabs on the pulse of society and react only when needed. Why is this analogy relevant? Because all of us have a heroic self trapped within us, but we lost contact with it when we unconsciously created our personal "Clark Kent" alter ego.

Our ego created our own "Clark Kent" as we grew older, and we have lost touch with the trapped hero that can achieve anything when unleashed. This is what the alter ego effect is all about. Using a method to unleash our true potential when the situation calls for it. I'm not suggesting you live full-time in an imaginary world (even though I would argue we are all doing it in the Matrix every single day). However, I am suggesting that there are times, especially on trail, when our best selves can't be found when we need them the most. An easy method to unleash this best version is to take on an alter ego when these obstacles present themselves. Let's look at a simple example from my youth.

When I was 12, I played war outside at night with my friend Doug. The goal was to wait until it was pitch black outside, run around my house with toy guns, and sneak up on the other guy and shoot him before he could shoot you. I was damn good at this game (perhaps it portended my future profession), but as I hid in the dark, I remember my fears creeping up on me. Movies like *Friday the 13th*, *Halloween,* and *Nightmare on Elm Street* ruined most of us in this generation. The nighttime activities kids enjoyed during those years were shaped by the experiences we saw on the screens of these scary films. I could fend off the fears seeping into my mind for a little while, but the longer I stayed hiding in the dark waiting for Doug, the stronger my fears swelled in my mind. As I hid deep inside the bushes, I kept hearing someone sneaking up on me from behind. In my mind, it was obviously either Freddy or Jason. I knew for a fact that it wasn't Doug . . . he truly sucked at playing war at night.

I also knew that if my fear forced me to move, even just a little, Doug would find me and win. So, how did I stay completely still while my mind raced out of control with the fear that Jason was about to chop me up into pieces with his machete? I turned myself into Rambo. I imagined I was this brave warrior hiding out in the woods as swarms of police chased me down. I could unleash my own courage by calling on the courage I saw Rambo display on screen. The fear was still there, but it became manageable in those moments. Luckily, Doug would soon run by and I would smoke his ass once again! However, without me summoning the courage of a movie character, Doug would have enjoyed many more victories that night.

Why did this Rambo technique work so well? Because I overrode my elephant's fear response by employing my rider's rationality. My rider was the one enabling me to take on Rambo's courage in those moments, and it also convinced the elephant's emotions to shift from fear to courage as well. I bolstered my faltering courage by acting like a courageous personality I admired. It's problem-solving 101. It's giving you the ability to overcome the parts of your disposition that keep you tethered to the sidelines. The parts that stymie your performance because of self-created mental obstacles. It's a method to bring out the traits inside you that exist but often lie dormant because your ego has channeled your behavior down a narrow corridor.

I don't want to give you the impression that you should use this only in times of fear or anxiety. There are times when our egos create obstacles in our path that are as large as anything nature can throw in front of us. Using an alter ego in those moments can help us show up with a better version of ourselves when the circumstances dictate. It can extract the traits that we possess at a deeper level but rarely use. Here is another example to help explain the concept a bit more.

Imagine you have been hiking around a couple of hikers for a few weeks and have grown close to them. Now imagine one of them is thinking about quitting his hike because he just received some unpleasant news from home. If you are anything like me, it's hard to be the empathetic person they need at that moment. To be the person who can connect with them, listen actively and deeply, and help them sort out their feelings by being there for them. It makes me sweat just thinking about it. Not because I don't care or don't want to help, but because my ego has spent a lifetime trying not to project what it feels is weakness (even though I know deep down inside that it's not). I often beat myself up mentally because I miss opportunities to help people needing some empathy from me. It's just not my strong suit and I have little practice at it because I have avoided those situations at all costs.

Luckily for me, my mom and wife are super effective at being there with a shoulder to cry on when people need it. Therefore, when put into a situation like the one above, I can simply draw on their empathetic traits and do what comes so naturally to them. This helps prevent my ego's attempts at suppressing my empathetic traits from appearing and allows me to be more supportive of someone in need. By taking on the alter egos of my mom and wife, I can turn myself into what this hiker needs in the moment. The traits were there all along, I just needed the means to extract them from their hiding spot. If we rely on our ego in these instances, we will fail to give the people in our lives the support they need. If we can take on someone else's traits that are hard for us to project with our normal personality, then we can nudge our rider, coax our elephant, and shape our path more effectively.

Where did this idea come from? I wish it were a theory that I created, but as it usually happens, I listened to a podcast with a guest talking about this concept. Intrigued, I read his book titled, *The Alter Ego Effect*. The concept floored me because it's such a powerful solution to problems I have been facing my entire adult life. Todd Herman is the author's name, and he is a performance coach in the sports and business world. He uses this technique to increase the performance of many elite athletes by enabling them to unleash the traits that are not inherently available to them.

In his book, Todd tells a story about meeting Bo Jackson a few minutes before stepping on stage to talk to an audience full of coaches. After some pleasantries, their conversation turned to Todd's work on the alter ego effect. Bo looked at Todd and said,

"Bo Jackson never played a down of football in his entire life."[32] Bo revealed he used an alternate ego on the field to prevent his normal anger and rage from manifesting in the game. This anger and rage caused him to make unforced penalties and created a distraction for his teammates.

But here is the most unique piece to Bo's story . . . his alternate personality was Jason. Yes, the same Jason from the *Friday the 13th* movies chasing me in the bushes as I waited for Doug on those dark nights in my youth. Why did Bo take on the alter ego of a masked serial killer? Because he saw Jason as emotionless, and Bo knew his emotions served as the biggest obstacle in his own life. By acting like Jason, Bo was hoping to suppress his rage on the football field. Did it work? Well, he is the only athlete in history to all-star in major league baseball and also play in the NFL Pro Bowl. So yes, I would say it worked. It's also important to note that Bo only took the parts of Jason that he needed, and, luckily, left the rest of the "murdering people with machetes" parts behind.

Hopefully, the question plaguing your mind right now is, How in the world will any of this help me on my long-distance hike? Well, when we face those difficult moments on trail that seem to attack the weak points of our nature, we can simply use the alter ego effect as a tool to overcome these obstacles. I have used this technique on my hikes since I read this book, and it works amazingly. Who are the personas I typically use in those moments? It depends on the situation. When I am hiking big-mile days of 25 miles or more, and my mind starts to waiver, or my body pushes back against me, I ask myself the question: "What would Hawk do right now?" If you don't know who Hawk is, check out his website https://www.craighawkmains.com/. He has thru-hiked the AT five times, vlogged four of them on YouTube, and is currently (as of July 2021) heading northbound on his sixth attempt. He is a beast on trail and can hike high-mileage days like he was put on this earth to do so.

The thing I respect most about Hawk is his ability to push through mental challenges with ease. I fancy myself as a mental guru most days, but to be honest, there are days I struggle more than most would assume. Therefore, when those times hit, I call on the traits of Hawk to remind me of how I should conduct business on trail in those moments. When I need the beast-mode ER to come out, I turn myself into Hawk in my mind until I get my elephant back on the right path. I tap into his grit, fortitude, and mental strength to suppress the diva that is trying to sneak into my head. Hawk is a freaking beast, and he helps remind me that I am too. Here is the best part, so don't miss it . . . IT NEVER FAILS!!!

I've had many people comment on my social media channels that they do something similar and use me as their alter ego in times of hardship on trail. That is super flattering and humbles me to no end. "Whatever it takes to take the next step" should be our motto as we begin any long-distance journey. There will be many days where our elephant is acting like a whiny bitch and we don't feel we have the internal resources to deal with the obstacles confronting us. That's when you need to employ whatever tool it takes to keep moving forward. The answer to all our problems on trail is forward movement. The only thing that quietens the elephant's tantrums is to push forward despite his emotional outbursts. To keep showing him that you are in charge, not him.

To prepare yourself to use the alter ego effect, you need to understand when it's most needed. For a good majority of hikers, the physical challenges in the first few weeks will probably require an alter ego at some point. It will seem as if you don't have the physical stamina to keep moving forward over the relentless mountains in your path. That's when you need to find the person in your life that exudes the grit the situation requires and turn yourself into them in your mind. (I often use the alter ego of former SEAL, and badass ultrarunner David Goggins. If you don't know who he is, you should look him up.) Ask yourself, How would they act and behave in these moments of challenge? Once you answer that question in your head, turn their behaviors into your behaviors. Unleash their traits from inside you. Get up that steep incline by using the stamina and grit of someone like Hawk who seems like he is walking on flat ground as he ascends those steep climbs. And once you get to the top of the climb, let Hawk go (or whoever your alter ego was) and turn back into you if that's what the moment calls for.

Conversely, during the times I know I should slow down and sit at an overlook with an expansive view, I ask myself "What would philosopher Alan Watts do right now?" The answer is always to stop and contemplate the beauty of life in this moment . . . and that's exactly what I do. Without asking myself this question, the underlying anxiety of "I need to get moving" will overtake my desire to sit still and enjoy the moment (dopamine in action). Turning my mind into Alan Watts overrides that anxiety and allows me to soak in life's stillness for a few minutes on those mountaintops (serotonin in action). I simply do what I assume he would do in that same situation, and voilà, it brings out the stillness that I had inside. I engender the traits my ego tries to suppress. I am telling you folks, this technique is so effective it's almost a travesty more humans aren't using it.

Be forewarned, your real ego won't like this technique much. It will tell you that you are perfect, and you don't need a silly alter ego to live your life. This is normal. However, don't be concerned about how silly it may seem to call on the traits of a cartoon character, a villain, an actor, a military hero, or a person from your own life to get you through the hard times on trail. (No one will know you are using this technique but you.) This isn't about devaluing who you are as a person. It's about realizing that we all struggle mentally at times and our ego has suppressed many of the traits that would help us get past some of life's obstacles.

If you fear heights, turn yourself into a person who shows no fear in the face of heights. If you fear being alone, turn yourself into someone that thrives when alone. If you fear being called upon for traits like empathy and compassion, turn yourself into someone who has deep empathy and compassion skills. If you do this effectively, your elephant will be easier to tame and your rider will have fun taking on the traits of these other people. In the end, I promise you will thank me (and Todd Herman) for this simple but effective strategy to overcome these mental obstacles.

Here is one last point that I want you to keep in mind when discussing the use of alter egos. We know that our thoughts affect our biology and that can be a positive or a negative. Therefore, I suggest when you choose your alter ego, try to choose people who bring positivity with them. Why? Because taking on egos that are focused on negativity will inadvertently flood our systems with the same negativity. Pointing back to Hawk, he is a good human that has a genuine positive disposition. Taking on his traits when I need them also brings with it his positive emotions. Win-Win. This doesn't mean there aren't times I lean on an ego like David Goggins when I need a kick in the ass. He has a perfect personality for it. But David's motivational drivers focus more on negative thoughts to push him down the course of his journey. For me, these are good for short bursts, but I don't want this negativity to be a continuous source of motivation for me. I want to use positivity to serve as the wind in my sails, not negativity that anchors me to past slights and hurt feelings.

That is the secret to the title of this book. "Pushing North" symbolizes my struggle with my mind and how I had to fight through the chaos the whole way to Katahdin. As discussed throughout the book, our biology reveals that negative-charged emotions release stress chemicals like cortisol and adrenalin into our system. These are good for short-duration threats, but not helpful for long-term health. They keep us hyper-alert and looking for more threats and this is not where I want to be mentally during my hike.

As we have learned, positive emotions release chemicals such as dopamine, serotonin, and oxytocin, all of which help us to buffer stress, sleep more soundly, be absorbed in the present moment, and feel connected with everything around us. Therefore, the final question we must ask ourselves as we employ this technique of using alter egos is, Do we want positive or negative dispositions entering our mental landscape? I'm nudging all of you to lean towards positivity as much as possible in your journey and your life.

Chapter Fifteen
Trail Time is Not Matrix Time

Time is a storm in which we are all lost.

William Carlos Williams

There is a truth on trail that isn't discussed much off trail. It's one of those mystical laws of nature that you don't waste time discussing with others that haven't experienced it for themselves. It's this intuitive sense that the other person won't be able to grasp the intricacies of what you are describing because they are void of the underlying framework. It's like trying to tell someone how to play the guitar when they've never seen a guitar.

Those lucky enough to have been initiated into this truth appreciate this dilemma of not understanding . . . because we all started there as well. This truth created a new level of self-awareness in my life that is hard to explain to those who haven't lived its precepts for months on end. This awareness has altered the very fabric of how I process my experiences after my indoctrination into its guiding principles. Let me try to explain.

When observing most accomplished long-distance hikers, several things stand out referencing how they are processing the world around them. They don't seem to be wrapped up in the same nonsense that the rest of us are struggling with. As I became hooked on watching thru-hiking videos in 2016, what stood out the most is that the hikers were not experiencing time in the same manner as I was inside the Matrix. They appeared to have this monk-like patience that seemed out of place inside our world of clocks and schedules. They didn't seem consumed with rushing around affixed to an agenda and trying to maximize every second of their day. This made little sense to me as an outsider looking into the world of long-distance hiking. I had to question whether I was actually seeing something different in them, or if I simply wanted to believe there was something different about how they managed time.

Over the next few months, I watched countless videos of thru-hikers hiking America's long trails and kept witnessing this same trait stretching across most of the hikers I watched. Something was changing inside them the farther they made it up the trail. They seemed to grow more and more patient as their journey unfolded. It looked appealing to me. It also looked foreign to me. As a self-proclaimed clock addict, I honestly couldn't decipher how hiking for days, weeks, and months could change how people processed time. A minute is still 60 seconds whether you are on a long-distance trail or deep inside the Matrix. In my conditioned mind, what I was seeing unfolding on YouTube made little sense . . . but it was alluring as hell.

This became the inception point of how I was "called" to the trail. It was like something deep inside wanted to find what I witnessed those hikers experiencing. To unshackle my life from the fake concept of time humans created to make managing the Matrix easier. For someone like me who is very conscientious and ordered, I've bought into the fallacy of time as much as anyone out there. But in 2016, I finally woke up enough to realize I wanted to let it go. I hadn't figured out how walking a long trail was going to help me release my grip on the comfort of time, but honestly, I had no better options.

Time was always one of those variables I felt I was controlling, but finally realized it's just a fallacy we tell ourselves. For those audiobook addicts out there, you already experience this perception when you choose how you listen to your book. For those unfamiliar, Audible gives the listener the option to choose a playback speed for the book they are listening to. Some prefer to listen at a speed of 1.5 (1.0 being normal speed), which increases the narrator's rate of speech and decreases the time it takes to listen to the entire book. We get to feel like we are fast-forwarding life with a push of a virtual button on a phone screen. We do this with many other areas in our lives as well.

We fast-forward through the boring parts of a show on Netflix, we take any shortcut available to reduce the time spent on a tedious project, we pull into a drive-thru because shopping and cooking take too much time, and we speed to our next destination because the drive seems boring and such a waste of our day. We do everything we can to reduce the time we have to spend in the dull parts of our experience. We just want to jump ahead to the good parts and bypass all the time that seems worthless to us. This defines Matrix time.

Matrix time was ruling my life leading up to my AT hike, but I thought I was the one in control. I felt I could manipulate the clock because I was in control of my actions. I thought by maximizing my schedule, I was making time benefit me. Wow, how ridiculous that sounds now. When we tell ourselves these silly stories, we convince ourselves we're in control. Folks, let me be clear, we are in control of nothing inside the Matrix. I finally discovered Matrix time is just an illusion. It just took me 2,000 miles of hiking to figure it out.

Hikers can learn to let go of their clinging to the clock during a long-distance hike. It won't be easy for most, but I argue it's where much of our mental freedom lies. When stepping on trail each morning, most hikers have a strategy for where they plan on ending their hike for the day. I was usually aiming somewhere in the 22 to 25-mile range. My rider would look ahead in that mileage bracket and get an idea of what the terrain would be like, what the water intervals were, and good places to camp later in the evening. He was like an internal drill sergeant that liked things to run on schedule. However, my elephant would remain anxious for most of the hiking day because he didn't enjoy the distances the rider wanted to travel. The elephant just wanted to fast-forward to the end of the day so it could avoid experiencing the pain, suffering, and boredom of hiking these big miles. Therein lies the conflict that Matrix time injects into our experience. The rider's plan depends on the clock and meeting timelines, while the elephant often sees time as a threat that creates suffering.

It was the overlap of these two entities inside my mind that caused much of my mental chaos as I headed north on the AT. Here is how the conversation often goes throughout the day . . . over, and over, and over again.

My rider: "It's almost nine o'clock and you have only done eight miles, you need to pick up the pace."

My elephant: "There is no way I want to hike this far today. My feet hurt, my back hurts, my shoulder hurts, and I am freaking exhausted. Can't we just slow down? Maybe we can catch a ride at the next road crossing and head into town for a day or two."

My rider: "Let's look at our watch again and see what time it is. Open the Guthook app and let's see how far we have gone since the last time we looked at it 10 minutes ago."

My elephant: "Yes, open Guthook and let's see how much farther we have to hike today. I just want it to be over so I can eat, lay in the tent, and relax. I am praying there aren't more big climbs."

My rider: "Ugh . . . I can't seem to maintain the desired three miles an hour pace due to all these blowdowns across the trail. I need to figure out a way to move faster so we can still make our mileage goal."

My elephant: "Can't someone come out here and clean this section up? See, I told you we should've gone into town. This is torture having to climb over all these fallen trees. How much longer are we going to keep doing this?"

Both of their arguments revolve around one thing . . . the concept of Matrix time. The rider is trying to use time as a tool to ensure he meets the goals he established for the day, and the elephant uses it as a measurement of pain, suffering, and misery. The rider gets frustrated when his efforts to control the clock don't go as planned because of variables outside his control. Fallen trees, excessive rocks, hot weather, thunderstorms, a lack of water, hard climbs, and steep down climbs all weigh negatively against the schedule he set for the day. He keeps checking the time to see how he's measuring up against his plan. He keeps pushing hard physically to stay on schedule. The elephant is already prone to anxiety, but add in a frustrated rider, and you have the recipe for a mental storm that will create chaos inside your mind . . . all day long.

It's also important to remember that our rider has limited energy available each day. His desire to push relentlessly towards his goal (dopamine in action) often triggers the elephant and creates mental friction. Once the rider loses his energy stores, you are left at the mercy of a triggered, emotional, 6-ton elephant who is thinking like a 5-year-old for the rest of the day. All this occurs because we are beholden to our innate concepts of Matrix time, even when we try to leave the Matrix behind.

It takes one of two things for this not to be true anymore: 1) deliberate effort to unlearn this ingrained habit of Matrix time, or 2) hike long and far enough so the experience itself redefines your concept of time. These aren't mutually exclusive choices. In fact, I argue they depend on each other in many ways. As we have discussed previously, it takes focused effort to change a habit, but it also takes time. How hard do you think it is to change something that is also a key variable to the change itself? Or asked differently, How can I let go of time when I depend on time to give me the experience I need to let it go? Yep, pretty damn difficult.

I was horrible at letting go of Matrix time during my hike. It was so ingrained inside my mind that I felt super uncomfortable when I tried to let my day flow naturally. I am one of those who fight the current and tries to keep the familiar parts of the shoreline in sight. What did this look like on my hike? It looked like me checking my watch dozens of times a day to see how I was doing on time. My rider loved making time-distance calculations to measure his worth. It looked like me opening my Guthook app many times an hour to check how far to the next water, how far have I been, how steep is this mountain I am ascending, and on, and on, and on.

Does this sound like an environment where Matrix time was dying, and the universe's time was taking over? Nope. How do you think my elephant was handling all the focus on what's next? Yep, you guessed it, he stayed triggered pretty much all day. As I mentioned earlier, once my rider fell offline due to a lack of energy, my elephant would wreak havoc inside my head for the rest of the afternoon. He injected a torrent of thoughts that weren't helpful at all. He turned a beautiful hike into a long and torturous afternoon of self-loathing and misery.

What did these afternoons look like as I hiked without a rider in control? Comments on my YouTube videos would make me angry, the terrain in front of me would trigger my inner diva, I wouldn't take care of my body as deliberately as I should have (I wouldn't eat or drink enough to keep up with the demand on my body), the bugs would torture me, the heat would send me into a mental hell, I would question why I was out here suffering, and these are but a few of the negative experiences my whiny elephant would create. All because my rider triggered him with his Matrix-time calculations that NEVER considered what the elephant needed to feel satiated.

I feel it necessary to remind you that this is MY experience and context. This is how my elephant and rider interacted inside my head on my AT hike. Some of you will relate to this, while others won't gain a sense of commonality from my descriptions. Those in the latter category have a little more work to do to connect the dots. I am imploring you to avoid convincing yourself this isn't happening inside of your mind just because you aren't relating to my experience. You must turn the spotlight on yourself and figure out how these elements are controlling your mental landscape.

Some of you will have a rather opposite experience. Your rider won't be as active and forceful as mine. Your elephant may play a much larger role in crafting how you use your time each day. Your elephant may play the "smiles before miles" script in your head which gives you the excuse to lay there a little longer before getting out of your tent to hit the trail. He may convince you that eight miles are good enough for the day, even though the deadline to reach Katahdin is looming in the not-so-distant future. He nudges you to ignore the rider's pleas to do more miles today to ease some anxiety later. Yes, for some out there, the rider is an outsider for most of the day and the elephant remains firmly in charge.

Honestly, this sounds horrible to me because it's not my lived experience, but I know it is for many. For many of you, your elephant is firmly in control of how you use your 24 hours in a day, and it's important to recognize this. Now that we have outlined both ends of the spectrum when contemplating how the rider and elephant control our time, I want to pull us below the surface and discuss what's hiding underneath.

Time is a prison for our minds. Time is this elusive measuring stick that we use to measure everything in our experience on trail. No one reading this will be free of its grasp on your hike, even though many convince themselves they are. But all of us can reduce its influence over our experience, we just have to figure out ways to loosen its grip.

With me being on the "my rider is firmly in control of my time" end of the spectrum, it took reaching Maine to realize I needed to take control over this beast running my life. Let me say that differently so the point is not lost. It took me 2,000 miles of hiking alone with myself to realize that my rider was guiding my obsessive focus on time. (This is why you must stay on your journey for the entire distance. Many of the lessons are waiting for you near the end.) How did I reduce the rider's over-reliance on Matrix time on the AT? I became disciplined about how I used the measuring stick.

As I drank my coffee in my tent each morning, I would do a quick scrub of the distance I wanted to travel, the terrain I would have to traverse to get there, and then I placed my watch and phone in my backpack and set a rule that I could only look at them during lunch. I had no way to measure my progress during the day except by using trail time. Let me tell you, we should ALL be living by trail time!!!

Trail time is just a fancy way to describe the natural cycles of the universe. The earth orbiting the sun. The moon orbiting the earth. Day shifting into darkness, and then back again. The tides rising and falling. The seasons increasing in intensity and then slowly giving way to the next with no seam in between. The rising and falling of the breath. The steady beating of our hearts. ALL OF IT! These are the natural rhythms of everything in the universe and I argue there was never a need to add Matrix time on top of this already perfect system.

As humans often do, we had to make things complicated. We allow Matrix time to control our lives from the moment we wake up to the second we fall asleep. We created an environment where productivity and stress became badges of honor. Our reward for this lifestyle is rampant cardiovascular disease, which is the leading cause of death in humans every year. All because we let Matrix time become our master. However, if we can get on trail and open ourselves fully to the experience, we can learn to let go of this make-believe measurement that has been imprisoning us our entire lives. We must simply hike long enough and far enough to allow the shift to happen. And when it does, you will never be the same again.

What does living by trail time feel like? I think it's different for everyone, but for me, it felt like I had opened my backpack and removed a 30-pound rock from it. It felt like someone took the blinders from my eyes and I could see the world from a new perspective. I felt lighter as I climbed those rugged mountains in Maine. My mind was much clearer, and I could focus more intently on the here and now. I could soak in the world around me for the first time since I left Springer. It was like bathing in a bath of serotonin and endorphins. Even though my body was exhausted from all the challenges it took to reach Maine, my energy levels seemed to be recharged. Instead of wasting tons of energy on calculations like "I need to move faster so I can make the next road in an hour," I was able to reallocate my energy towards focusing on the present moment and finding gratitude for the journey.

Maybe a good question to answer to help clarify this concept is, What does Matrix time feel like when compared to trail time? Matrix time feels like suffering; trail time feels like coherence. Matrix time feels hurried, impatient, and heavy; trail time feels like a smooth flowing stream that carries no weight whatsoever. If you are suffering, if you feel anxious, if you feel heavy, then I can almost guarantee you are caught in the tentacles of Matrix time. If you are too restless to sleep, depressed, anxious, uptight, impatient, edgy, worried, and all the other hundreds of descriptors I could list here, I can guarantee Matrix time is a culprit in some fashion. When we stop measuring everything with seconds, minutes, hours, and days, we realize the universe has its own measurements for time that are perfect.

As trail time began to drive my experience on the AT, it helped me appreciate all the moments we fast-forward through in the Matrix. When you step on trail in the morning and plan on hiking 12 to 20 miles for the day, those still wrapped inside Matrix time will feel a sense of anxiety and impatience. They will long for the end of the day to be here so they can avoid the suffering that awaits them on their path. They look forward to the views but loathe the distance in between each mountain top. Anytime they descend, they are already dreading the next climb. Anytime they are halfway up a long climb, they are looking as far up ahead as possible in hopes to catch a glimpse of sunlight through the trees symbolizing they must be near the summit. Anytime they see a difficult stretch of trail ahead of them on Guthook, the temptation to yellow blaze often lures them in (yellow-blazing is skipping portions of the trail). It's as if they feel they still have that remote control in their hand and try to fast-forward through the parts of life they see as boring or painful—just like on Netflix.

Don't mishear me, even after I had my "trail-time epiphany," my rider still tortured me to provide him some means of measuring our progress. Without these measurements, he felt he couldn't conduct his problem-solving calculations. I still endured a triggered elephant in the late afternoons when I was miles from where I'd hoped to camp that night. But by placing my Matrix measuring tools (my watch and phone) in my backpack and shaping the path in front of me, I robbed both the rider and elephant of their link into the stress-filled world of time. I forced them to use trail time, and eventually, they quit resisting.

Adaptation is rarely easy. As we talk about adapting ourselves to a reality outside of Matrix time, we can also use the tools discussed in this book to reduce the negative effects this adaptation will create on our rider and elephant. Focusing on the bright spots of the day serves to suppress the rider's focus on solving all the negative problems he finds in the environment surrounding him. If we can interrupt his search for problems, suddenly, there are no problems.

Looking back, I found these bright spots much easier when I redirected my focus away from Matrix time. Each view took on a new meaning. Each change in scenery seemed to reach deeper into my soul. I can remember one spot in Maine where the trail took on a primitive coniferous ambiance that made me feel like I had just entered a medieval forest. It stayed this way for a few miles and I became engrossed in the environment. Each tree drew my attention towards its massive beauty, the roots covering the trail became more like artwork than a nuisance, the soil had the aroma of what I imagined heaven would smell like when I was a child, and the air coming into my lungs felt like it was energized with electricity that kept feeding the desire to move forward and see what was around the next bend. Finding the bright spots around you does one simple but powerful thing . . . it helps you find more bright spots.

Once we can subdue our rider's incessant search for problems to solve, our elephants have more space to employ their positive emotions in our day. As we find those bright spots, our elephants can now bolster those moments with serotonin and dopamine. The serotonin helps to absorb us into the present moment and the dopamine keeps us wanting to find more of it. Without all the negative perceptions from our rider, the elephant can enter a present-moment playground and explore his surroundings with curiosity, wonderment, and awe. Without Matrix time swarming us like a horde of gnats, we can now reduce the friction our conditioned thoughts have created in our lives. It's no longer "I need to get 25 miles in before six o'clock tonight," but more of "I can't wait to see what's between me and wherever I decide to stop this evening." Every step becomes a new adventure. Every mountain feels like home. All because our elephant is no longer triggered by the conditions of Matrix time and our rider has turned into a bright-spot finding machine.

I can't close this chapter out without reminding the reader that most of these life-altering revelations aren't available in the early stages of these long-duration events. On the AT, I consider everything before Vermont an early stage. Others may disagree with that measurement and that's OK because the lessons manifest at different times for each of us. But the fact remains, the longer you stay on trail, the better chance the trail will unveil the lessons you need to evolve as a human. What I love about this concept is that it's not a Matrix-type problem where you can throw money at the predicament and sidestep the obstacles. Like author Ryan Holiday said in his book *The Obstacle is the Way*, "The obstacle in the path becomes the path. Never forget, within every obstacle is an opportunity to improve our condition."[33]

It's only when we confront and overcome these obstacles that we experience growth. Matrix time does nothing but create friction on our path and anchors us to anxiety and fear. Until we can learn to let it go during our journey, we will face the same friction as we do in our normal lives. We will always search for an easier path around the obstacles in front of us. Eventually, three out of four of us will drop off trail well before we learn the most valuable lessons the trail had awaiting us.

Here is the last question for this chapter, How do you know when your adaptation to trail time is complete? I argue, it's when your rider and elephant are no longer serving as anchors . . . but have transformed into sails. It's when we can finally recognize Matrix time as the prison it truly is. It's when you can flow with the rhythm of nature during your day and leave the anxiety, fear, and restlessness of the Matrix world behind. It's when all the miles between you and your destination no longer seem like torture, but appear as gifts.

Chapter Sixteen
Breathe

Your mind, emotions, and body are instruments, and the way you align and tune them determines how well you play life.

Harbhajan Singh Yogi

To undertake a journey that demands an extreme physical output, we rely on our body to bear the burden and get us from point A to point B. As mentioned earlier in the book, our breathing, digestion, heartbeat, temperature, and many more bodily functions are controlled for us, so we don't have to waste precious mental energy on them. This homeostasis—our body's synchronization of all the processes to keep it functioning at a baseline level—is thankfully moderated by our autonomous nervous system. However, when we expect our bodies to perform in conditions outside of this homeostasis (like on a challenging journey), we must employ the tools of our rider and elephant to increase our chances of success. Therefore, we need to figure out which bodily functions we can commandeer and use in our favor. If we can make these functions work to our advantage, we can increase our performance during these long hikes and be more present throughout the experience.

Arguably, the most beneficial bodily function nature offered us control over is our breathing. Somewhere throughout our evolution, we were given control of the skeletal muscle that can inflate and deflate our lungs on command. This muscle also aggravates the crap out of us when it starts to spasm—AKA the hiccups. The diaphragm, in all its skeletal muscle glory, gives us conscious control over our breathing and can serve as a governor for our central nervous system if we learn how to use it correctly. What an amazing opportunity we were provided with this tool. Left alone, our autonomous system takes control of the diaphragm and lets it do what it does best . . . keep us alive. However, when we learn to control it effectively, we open a doorway to a world of increased awareness and performance in our lives. There has been a ton of solid research completed around breathing and how it can help us not only survive . . . but thrive.

Maybe the most beneficial function our diaphragm offers is the ability to kick-start our parasympathetic nervous system (rest and digest system) during times of stress. The simple technique of diaphragmatic breathing—controlled deep breaths which bring in more oxygen and expels higher levels of carbon dioxide from the body—helps lower our heart rate and stabilize our blood pressure.[34] The most exciting benefit of breath control is that it has been scientifically proven to reduce the negative effects of stress. Most of all, it's available to all of us. It's biology, not personality. It's a technique we can use to bring our emotional elephant back on course when things go sideways.

This is a tool that can work rapidly. It's a technique that many elite athletes use to level their bubbles between plays, and a tool many SOF operators use to gain mental clarity in those last few seconds before the explosive breach goes off and they enter an enemy-held building. It allows us access to a healthier headspace without having to do the traditional "I have to go for a long run to clear my head," or the "I need a few drinks to quieten the thoughts in my mind" routines we so often rely upon. The only requirement to access this tool is awareness. Unfortunately, this awareness is often the one thing most of us lack in our daily lives inside the Matrix.

Hopefully, this book has offered some tools that help you open your awareness and recognize when your mind is creating chaos. Anything can trigger this chaos and it's impossible to stop every occurrence from happening. Our brains are running full-time in the background. They are thought-manifesting machines. Therefore, we must be self-compassionate with ourselves when the chaos appears.

If we can recognize the chaos is happening before it causes too much damage, we can change the trajectory of the experience and get our rider and elephant back on the desired path. We can do this through our breath and the fastest and most simple method is through the physiological sigh. This technique is a pattern of breathing where two inhales through the nose are followed by an extended exhale through the mouth.[35] This method works great when we need to gain control over our stress response quickly. It's like pressing the brakes on a car speeding out of control.

How do we do a physiological sigh? We start by inhaling (through the nose works best) a large volume of air into our belly. Without releasing, we will pause for a brief second and then take in one more breath of air. Once complete, we will then slowly exhale fully from our mouth to a count of six to eight. When we repeat this several times, it triggers our parasympathetic response. It puts the breaks on our amygdala's attempts at creating more chaos in our mind and body. You can do this at any point in your day. It's available to you free of charge, but you must have the awareness to know that you need it.

This breathing technique should look somewhat familiar to you.

We all experienced it as a child when we started crying uncontrollably and began sucking in air in the same pattern we are talking about with a physiological sigh. If you are a parent, you are familiar with this in your children. It's their body trying to override their sympathetic stress response by getting the parasympathetic system engaged. Much like the alter ego effect, the physiological sigh is another tool we intuitively used as children but failed to bring with us into adulthood.

Why does this technique work? Stanford neurologist and researcher Andrew Huberman explains it like this: "You have little sacks of air in the lungs (alveoli), which increase the volume of air that you can bring in. Those sacks collapse over time, and as a result, oxygen levels start to go down and carbon dioxide levels go up in the bloodstream and body. The double inhales of the physiological sigh "pops" the air sacks open, allowing oxygen in and enabling you to offload carbon dioxide in the long exhaled sigh out."[36]

So, how does this apply to our world of long-distance hiking? We have already established that the most difficult aspect of these long-duration events is the mental side of the equation. You can guarantee that our stress response will be triggered many times a day and mental chaos will often follow. This may be caused by a dangerous fall where we bang ourselves up a bit, a thunderstorm on our heels, a hard climb up a ridiculously steep mountain, not making it to the post office in time to grab our resupply package, or our inability to accomplish the goals we established for ourselves during the day. Regardless of what causes the chaos to arise, we need to stop the mental friction our mind is creating sooner than later. The physiological sigh is a great technique to use in these moments of mental chaos, but prevention should be our long-term goal during our journeys. The more stable our mental landscape remains, the more energy we will have available for experiencing things like joy, wonder, awe, and fulfillment.

Over the past three years, meditation has provided a sturdy mental foundation for me. When we discuss meditation it creates one of several responses inside people that haven't experienced its potency. Some feel repelled by it, others are drawn to it, and some are dumbfounded by its prevalence in today's milieu surrounding peak performance. But if we break it down to its core facets, meditation is nothing more than awareness, breathing, and focus. That's it. There is nothing mystical about it, nothing to fear, nothing to be embarrassed about. It's simply a period where we open our awareness, we breathe, and we focus on our breaths. But wait . . . if it's nothing more than awareness, breathing, and focus, how will that help anything?

The biggest benefit I feel meditation offers is the ability to bring our awareness and focus back to the body when the mind creates false narratives in our heads. It's during these moments that our mind detaches from our body and moves to the past or future. Regardless of which direction it travels, it leaves our body to fend for itself. We lose the ability to take control of our breath through our diaphragm, and our disjointed thoughts create a fictional narrative that often triggers the stress response. This response launches a cocktail of cortisol and adrenalin into our system . . . and starts fueling the chaos inside. The cure to this infliction is as simple as awareness, breathing, and focus. But these simple remedies elude most of us because we get ensnared by these past or future narratives. Our goal with meditation is to enable ourselves to become aware when we leave the present moment so we can come back to it.

What I have discovered through several years of dedicated meditation practice (15-20 minutes a day, first thing in the morning) is that I can more easily recognize when my mind is drifting away towards these false realities and refocus it back to my body. Once it's back to my body, I take control of my diaphragm for a few deep breaths to get my mind-body alignment back in order. From this state, my rider and elephant are much more compliant and easier to guide and control. In layman's terms, this means that I can better regulate my thoughts, emotions, and behaviors with this increase of awareness and focus. When my mind is trapped in a funnel of autonomic thoughts and false narratives, my rider and elephant are trapped as well. This results in my rider making terrible decisions that I may regret later, and my elephant remaining emotionally triggered when there is no real threat to speak of.

When the chaos is running rampant in our minds, most of us can't separate it from our true inner peace. We identify with the chaos even though it's a made-up fantasy of the conditioned mind. We often feel the only way to end the chaos is by removing ourselves from the environment. This is why so many people never finish anything hard. They just keep running from their chaotic thoughts. Hear this clearly . . . no matter what environment you place yourself in, the chaos will still find you. Quitting is not the solution . . . it's the surest way to incite years of pain, remorse, and more mental chaos. The only way to find peace, joy, and fulfillment is by finishing what we set out to do. To accomplish the goal.

To make this a reality, we must learn to overcome the chaos that is awaiting all of us. We must enable ourselves to see the friction as it's forming. To see our triggers before they ignite the spark. To avoid letting the rider and elephant be coerced into taking the wrong path. To keep our mental bubbles leveled more easily throughout our hiking day. To remember that our thoughts are nothing but a false projection on a screen in our heads.

This takes a level of awareness most of us don't possess in our normal lives. That's understandable because most of us don't realize there's a problem to begin with. We just ride the waves of make-believe stress and emotions in our minds because it has always been that way. It's who we think we are. But here's the secret . . . it's all a fabrication. It's a made-up story we keep proliferating inside our minds. That's where meditation comes into the picture. It's a simple technique we can use to suppress these false narratives and bring our awareness back to the only time that exists . . . right here, right now. When we build a foundation of awareness and focus through meditation, we arm ourselves with the tools to arrest the chaos before it builds up steam. To bring our mind and body back into alignment and recenter our focus on our breath.

Here is the question I now ask each of you, How will you integrate meditation into your life? How will you use the lessons from meditation to pacify the elephant and direct the rider? Here's the secret . . . it doesn't take but a few minutes a day to reap the benefits of meditation. With mindfulness meditation—a form of meditation where you simply focus on your breath or the stimuli that your senses are taking in—the Mayo Clinic cites that as little as one minute can have positive effects.[37] In fact, like any habit, we need to start small and build from there. That's exactly what I did. I started with 10-minute guided meditation videos on YouTube and expanded from there. You can start even smaller if needed. The point is to find the time and do it.

YouTube or most other meditation apps give you the ability to dial in what works best for you. This is great because it robs us of the excuse matrix we try to employ when we start a new habit. Find what works for you and move towards it. The choices are many. Do you prefer to meditate in silence? With background music playing? With someone's voice guiding you to help keep you focused? Do you like a male voice or a female voice? Do you want nature scenes playing on the screen during the session? Do you want to spend 10 minutes doing it? 15? 30? All these choices are available. Quit considering if you should try it and just do it. You can thank me later for the life-changing effects you will experience if you stick with it.

My practice is as follows: I wake up at three o'clock in the morning and settle into my reading chair with a mug of coffee. I spend the first 15-20 minutes of my day establishing my mental foundation through meditation. I usually opt for guided meditation videos from YouTube and have progressed up to 20-minute sessions as of late. I have several standard videos I use exclusively now. For the last month or so I have been using several guided meditations by Mooji—a Jamaican spiritual teacher that conducts talks and retreats for those wanting to find their true selves. There is something magnetic about his delivery, voice, words, rate of speech, tone, and sense of understanding that draws me into a deep state of meditation. Twenty minutes go by fast when I am listening to a Mooji guided meditation, and I am usually somewhat sad when it comes to an end. That is a far cry from where I started when sitting still for 10 minutes felt like torture.

I seriously hope you will give meditation a shot in your life. If you are planning a long-distance hike or any other long-duration event, the question you must ask yourself is this: What do you have to lose? Any research-proven tool that can improve your focus, help regulate your emotions and behavior, and help calm the chaos inside your mind SHOULD be in your toolbox as you start pushing north. I promise you will need it on your journey.

Mouth Breathers Beware

Most humans are terrible at the act of basic breathing. Have you ever sat and listened to the people around you breathe? I'm not talking about while they are doing physical labor or exercise, I mean when they are just sitting around breathing. If you could hear them breathing, that is the first clue that something is already out of center. When I listen to people on a plane or in the airport, it amazes me how poorly people are intaking oxygen. People sound like they are lumbering just to get oxygen into their system and that is scary on so many levels. It's like a cacophony of human vacuum cleaners that have clogged filters and are struggling to bring in enough air to function. Another abnormality is the number of mouth breathers in the world. Show me a mouth breather and I will show you someone ineffective at the art of breathing.

Why does the way we breathe matter? Because it's the only biological tool nature gave us the ability to control. It's the one piece of life that we should all become experts at. When relating it to our long-distance journeys, our breath is often the only centerline we have when things go sideways. This means the more effective we breathe before things go haywire, the more likely we can recover and keep moving towards our goals.

The Nose is Key

Breathe through your nose. Why? Author and breath expert James Nestor reveals in his book *Breath*, that by simply breathing through our nose, we increase our oxygenation by 20 percent. Inhaling more oxygen allows us to breathe less. By breathing less, we slow down our heart rate. A reduction in heart rate reduces the burden on our hearts and decreases our blood pressure. Nose breathing also increases our endurance, our recovery, and helps fight off pathogens, bacteria, and viruses much more effectively.[38] It helps establish an effective centerline to return to when things get ramped up.

Become more aware of how you are bringing air into your body. Science has confirmed that breathing through our nose is the most efficient way to get oxygen into our system. If you are a habitual mouth breather, this may take some work to change, but the evidence suggests it's well worth the effort. If you have health issues that are creating the secondary effect of laborious breathing (e.g., overweight, out of shape, deviated septum, hypertension, etc.), you need to focus on fixing those underlying issues first.

For all those who will be climbing and descending many mountains during your long-distance hikes, tune into your breathing and ensure you use your nose as much as possible. I get it, there are times we are climbing an uber-steep trail and we need to suck in as much air as possible (through any orifice available), but those are the moments we need the awareness the most. We need to take a second to pause, bring in a couple of deep breaths into our nose, and bring our system down out of the red. I'm not saying there aren't times where it will be necessary to push ourselves hard on trail, but anytime we push our bodies into the red it comes at a significant downstream cost. That cost, as we have discussed throughout the book, is usually a depleted rider and a triggered elephant. Therefore, when we feel ourselves getting near the red, we need to take a moment and regain some breath composure by shifting our intake back to our nose.

On my AT hike, I prided myself on being able to reach most mountain tops without having to stop and pause to catch my breath on the way up. What this really meant is that I pushed myself into the red several times a day . . . for no reason other than pride and ego. Now that I understand the downstream cost of those decisions, I'm much more strategic with how I approach climbs. I focus on ensuring my pace still allows me to breathe through my nose as much as possible. When my heart rate increases, I will often exhale through my mouth, but I hold the line on the goal that my in-breaths MUST come in through my nose for all the reasons we discussed above. It's more efficient and helps reduce the cost the climb will have on my elephant and rider later in the day. It helps keep my elephant from waging war against me when I push myself into the red for no beneficial reason whatsoever. Just remember, any method to prevent our elephant from waging war inside our mental space is worth considering.

Focusing on our breath also brings our mind back to our body while hiking. It's a basic form of meditation. I try to use it strategically to bring my feet back under me—meaning to reset my mind-body alignment. When our rider loses energy during the late afternoons, our ability to focus on simple things like our breathing will be difficult. It's why those afternoon climbs are so torturous mentally. We lose the ability to coax our elephant. We feel like a walking zombie. Each step is hard, and each tiny hill feels like Everest. This is when you must shake yourself enough to come back to your breath. Take a moment, get some deep breaths in through your nose, get your feet back under you, and simply look around and think, "I don't have to do this . . . I get to do this." I suggest that more times than not, if you employ something similar, your afternoons will be more mentally tolerable, and your mind-body alignment will remain synchronized for much longer periods of time.

Chapter Seventeen
The Nature of it All

This universe is not outside you. Look inside yourself; everything that you want, you already are.

Rumi

Well, here we are at the last chapter. All I can hope for is that you are still reading and that some of the thoughts in this book will help you achieve whatever goals are on your horizon. However, there is still one piece of the puzzle left unplaced. This one is the most beneficial if you can grasp its meaning.

During your long and challenging journey, you will grow in ways that aren't obvious to you in each moment. They are happening slowly, and each step forward adds more experience and perspective to this growth. Each time you learn another technique to focus your rider back on your goals and nudge your elephant back onto the righteous path, you grow as a human. This growth is not there to help define you . . . definitions are constraining and limiting. No, this growth is meant to evolve you. To expand you. To tear down the boundaries of who you thought you were before you began your journey. To help you realize that there are no boundaries holding you back. There never have been. It's been your Matrix-conditioned mind that has served as your only obstacle your entire life. But now, you are learning to tear down those limitations and keep pushing north. Just one more step, then another, then another . . . there is no bigger secret than that.

I will now share an experience that happened to me during my AT hike that I have shared with no one. This event expanded my understanding of my place in the universe more than anything I have encountered in my 50 years of life . . . and it happened at a simple stop to refill my water.

I made it to a shelter that was just off trail, and it had a stream running nearby. I set my backpack down inside the shelter, grabbed my two water containers, and sat down next to this wonderful stream. There was plenty of water flowing, but there wasn't a spot where I could dip my bottle underneath an overhang and fill it directly. No problem, that's why we bring a little scoop with us (usually a bottom of a SmartWater bottle we cut for this very purpose).

As I started scooping water and transferring it into one of my bottles, my curiosity was running wide open in my mind. As I watched the water enter the scoop, and then the larger bottle, I began contemplating how the water wasn't resisting my efforts to remove some of its form from the creek. I was amazed at how it could take the new shape of the different containers I was placing it in. It simply molded itself to the scoop and bottles in perfect fashion and then integrated seamlessly with the existing water in the bottle as I poured it in. No anxiety, no stress, no friction . . . just formless and malleable. I must admit, scooping water was something that I had done dozens of times during my hike, but this time I could finally see the lesson hidden inside. Be like water.

Even though I would have been satisfied with that golden nugget of universal wisdom, it didn't end there. My mind kept searching for something else. There was an even bigger question looming, but I couldn't make it bubble to the surface. I sat there for a few minutes in a state of curiosity, playing gently in the water . . . and then it hit like a bolt of lightning. I dipped more water into my scoop, held it up to eye level, and stared at it. The question circulating in my head was, What is happening to the molecules, atoms, bacteria, and all the other millions of organisms that are now contained inside my scoop? The answer was obvious but wouldn't have entered my consciousness had I not asked the question. The water (meaning all those parts combining to create the water) was adapting, morphing, and growing to meet the demands of its new environment. At that moment, it became analogous to the journey I was experiencing on my thru-hike. I was that scoop of water in an unfamiliar environment, having to learn to adapt, morph, and grow to meet the demands of the trail. It was so obvious, yet it hadn't hit me as hard as it did at this moment.

But the true lesson still hadn't hit yet. As I sat there for 10 minutes staring at the water in the scoop and contemplating what was happening inside, another jolt of curiosity hit me . . . what happens when I pour the water back into the stream? How would this scoop of water, with its components that have morphed over the last few minutes to meet the demand of their new environment, interact with the larger body of water as I poured it back in?

The fact is, the water in the scoop was now different from the rest of the water in the stream. It has a new consciousness that none of the other organisms in the stream are familiar with. Therefore, when we pour it back in, the water from the scoop increases the intelligence of the original source because it has taken what it learned in the scoop and blended it back into the larger stream. One tiny scoop of water that went on a grand journey into my scoop for 10 minutes reentered the stream at a higher level of consciousness. It had been forced to adapt, to grow, to become more aware of the fact that it was a separate entity for a moment in time, then blended back into the whole.

At a smaller level, this is exactly what is happening to you as you experience your long-distance hike or some other long-duration event. You leave the world in which everything is familiar, comfortable, and easy, and enter an unfamiliar environment where you must adapt quickly, learn to survive, and keep finding novel ways to move forward. Inside this metaphorical scoop, you become something different. Your consciousness elevates. You transform into something that the outside world doesn't recognize easily.

On an existential level, the scoop metaphor is simply pointing to our meaning and purpose for the 70+ years we get to spend on this planet. We are now inside the "scoop," learning, growing, adapting, advancing, and moving forward. Once it's our turn to be poured back into the stream of the universe, we take with us a higher level of consciousness. We increase the intelligence of the universe by living the life it has blessed us with. This is the value of every living creature. Each life force allows the universe to bear witness to itself. To learn, to adapt, to grow, and to keep taking the next step forward.

You are a tiny but uber-important piece to the universe's puzzle of existence. By pushing yourself into uncomfortable positions of growth, you are filling in much larger swaths of the universal puzzle than those content to dwell in the comforts and safety of the Matrix. The universe needs us to push our limits during the short expanse of our life. It needs us to keep searching out the boundaries of our experience. Doing so adds value to the collective. It creates a universe that can evolve more quickly and effectively.

This is why this book is so important to me. It's why I argue it's so important for all of us. The more ships that launch from the harbor, the more likely a new horizon will be discovered. The more humans that stay on trail long enough to receive the lessons awaiting them, the more water that enters the scoop. The more water in the scoop, the bigger effect it has when we pour you back into society. And eventually, in the hopefully not-so-distant future, the course of the ship will change ever so slowly and carry us to a new horizon where we can live human principles, not Matrix principles. A horizon that leads us to unity as a species. A place where we have more control over the rider and elephant and can become better versions of ourselves every single day. Sound pollyannaish? Maybe. But I passionately believe that if we can break free of these fetters of the Matrix, anything is possible. We just need more of you in the scoop.

The last thing I want to discuss are the options available to us when we begin to feel those tinges of post-trail depression. We often find cures in the most obvious places, and I suggest if you take the time to define your meaning and purpose before your hike, the likelihood of you experiencing post-trail depression will be reduced significantly. Why? Because the meaning we established was pointing to something outside of ourselves. To something bigger than us. To something that still needs our focus and attention after our hike is complete.

To be honest, I have discovered over the last decade that I am someone who can fall into depression fairly easily. I never knew what it was, but when I experienced it for long periods, it reduced my world to this narrow little channel of suffering. The goal of aiming our meaning outside of ourselves is to aim the spotlight of awareness towards something that will incite action inside of us. When I got home from Maine, it was now time to try and apply the lessons from the trail that would hopefully make me a more present husband and father. There was no time to sit with the spotlight on me . . . I had to move towards my meaning. Was I perfect at it? HELL NO! I still made a bunch of mistakes, but I was focused and intent on trying, and that kept me moving forward. I fail, learn, and grow every single day, and my meaning still adds wind to my sails, four years later.

On top of my desire to be a better husband and father, the dedication to help the children at St. Jude kept my spotlight of focus on something much bigger than me as well. My YouTube channel (and a large donation by my wonderful sister) donated a sizeable chunk of cash to this wonderful charity. There was no time to look behind me and long to be back inside the scoop. No, the scoop was a gift and when we are poured back into the larger stream, it's time to make use of the lessons we were so blessed to receive. Our journey didn't end at the far terminus . . . it simply transformed. We leveled up and now it's our task to evolve with it. To find the meaning outside of ourselves and orient our energy and focus towards something bigger. To convince as many people as possible to leave their Matrix cage and enter the scoop as well.

I still offer the obligatory "If you are suffering from post-trail depression, seek professional help" advice. However, if you follow the lessons of this book, the likelihood you will have time for anything other than taking the next step forward becomes less likely. That's what this entire journey is about . . . finding the ability to nudge our minds and bodies to take one more step forward . . . and then another . . . and then another. Until it's our time to be poured back into the universe and we prepare for our next journey to begin. Quit wasting this life on trivial drivel. Shed off your Matrix bowlines, go grab your backpack, find a trail that will push you to your limits, apply the lessons in this book, and come join us in the scoop of life while you still can!

ABOUT THE AUTHOR

Trey (Early Riser) Free is a husband, father, retired special operations forces (SOF) operator, thru-hiker, author, and guide to those seeking to escape the Matrix. His first book, *It's Time to Choose, Your Ego or You*, revealed the driving force behind his search for the stillness we all have hiding deep inside. He exposed how dangerous and disrupting our egos prove to be in our lives and the realization that we must wake up or face a life plagued with self-induced misery and suffering. His passion to help guide others to the trailhead of self-awareness and stillness became the motivation behind *Pushing North*.

He currently lives in North Carolina with his wife Teresa, and their teenage son Caleb.

Follow him on social media at:

YouTube: Early_Riser_71
Instagram: earlyriser71
Facebook: early.riser.108 (Howard Free)

Sources and Websites

[1] Andrew Huberman, PhD. The Huberman Lab Podcast; Episode 6: *How to Focus to Change Your Brain.* https://hubermanlab.libsyn.com/how-to-focus-to-change-your-brain-episode-6

[2] E. Engl, and D Attwell. (2015), Non-signalling energy use in the brain. J Physiol, 593: 3417-3429. https://doi.org/10.1113/jphysiol.2014.282517

[3] Jonathan Haidt. (2006). *The Happiness Hypothesis.* Basic Books.

[4] Ibid.

[5] James Clear. *Atomic Habits.* Penguin Random House, New York, NY. 2018

[6] Ibid.

[7] VeryWellMind.com. Definition of perception. https://www.verywellmind.com/perception-and-the-perceptual-process-2795839#citation-2

[8] GN Kenyon, KC Sen. "The Perception Process". *The Perception of Quality*. Springer, London. 2015. doi:10.1007/978-1-4471-6627-6_5. https://link.springer.com/chapter/10.1007%2F978-1-4471-6627-6_5.

[9] David Eagleman. *The Brain: The Story of You.* Vintage Books, 2017.

[10] University of California Press, Collabra Psychology. "Standing in Awe: The Effects of Awe on Body Perception and the Relation with Absorption." https://online.ucpress.edu/collabra/article/2/1/4/112683/Standing-in-Awe-The-Effects-of-Awe-on-Body.

[11] Ibid.

[12] Brian Greene. Guest on the Joe Roan Experience. Spotify, Episode 1631. 8 April, 2021. https://open.spotify.com/episode/3Atye1uCqaW2Ver3d16wJO

[13] Ryan Holiday, Stephen Hanselman. *The Daily Stoic.* Penguin Publishing Group. Kindle Edition.

[14] John Milton. (1674). Paradise Lost; A Poem in Twelve Books (II ed.). London: S. Simmons.

[15] Judson Brewer, PhD. Rich Roll Podcast, Episode 586, "Breaking the Cycle of Worry and Fear." March 8, 2021. https://www.richroll.com/podcast/jud-brewer-586/

[16] Merriam Webster Dictionary. Definition of Habit. https://www.merriam-webster.com/dictionary/habit

[17] Andrew Huberman, PhD. The Huberman Lab Podcast; Episode 6: *How to Focus to Change Your Brain.* https://hubermanlab.libsyn.com/how-to-focus-to-change-your-brain-episode-6.

[18] Wharton Health Care Management Alumni Association. "The Neuroscience of Gratitude." https://www.whartonhealthcare.org/the_neuroscience_of_gratitude

[19] Ibid

[20] James Clear. *Atomic Habits.* Penguin Random House, New York, NY. 2018

[21] Andrew Huberman, PhD. Lex Fridman Podcast #164: "Sleep, Dreams, Creativity & the Limits of the Human Mind". 28 February, 2021. https://lexfridman.com/andrew-huberman-2/

[22] David Goggins. *Can't Hurt Me: Master Your Mind and Defy the Odds.* (pp. 210-211). Lioncrest Publishing. Kindle Edition.

[23] Kottler, p. 25.

[24] David Perlmutter, PhD. "How Your Sleep Affects Your Weight." Guest on the Health Theory Podcast; released 25 March 2021. Online at https://impacttheory.com/episode/dr-david-perlmutter/

[25] Ibid.

[26] Zach Davis. *Appalachian Trials: The Psychological and Emotional Guide to Successfully Thru-Hiking The Appalachian Trail.* Good Badger Publishing (February 1, 2012).

[27] Kotler. P. 27

[28] David Foster Wallace. *This is Water: Some Thoughts, Delivered on a Significant Occasion, About Living a Compassionate Life.* New York: Little, Brown. 2009

[29] Andrew Huberman, PhD. The Huberman Podcast. Ep 12: *How to Increase Motivation and Drive.* https://hubermanlab.libsyn.com/how-to-increase-motivation-drive-episode-12.

[30] Hormone Health Network. "Your Health and Hormones". https://www.hormone.org/your-health-and-hormones/glands-and-hormones-a-to-z/hormones/serotonin

[31] Lisa Rozak Burton. "The Neuroscience of Gratitude". Wharton Healthcare and Alumni Association. https://www.whartonhealthcare.org/the_neuroscience_of_gratitude.

[32] Todd Herman. *The Alter Ego Effect.* Harper Business (February 5, 2019).

[33] Ryan Holiday. *The Obstacle Is The Way: The Timeless Art of Turning Trials Into Triumph.* Portfolio/Penguin (2014).

[34] "Diaphragmatic Breathing." Johns Hopkins All Children's

Hospital, 2020, www.hopkinsallchildrens.org/Services/Anesthesiology/Pain-Management/Complementary-Pain-Therapies/Diaphragmatic-Breathing.

[35] Holly MacCormick. "How Stress Affects Your Brain and How to Reverse It." Scope, 7 Oct. 2020. https://scopeblog.stanford.edu/2020/10/07/how-stress-affects-your-brain-and-how-to-reverse-it/#:~:text=One%20breathing%20pattern%20they're,that%20you%20can%20bring%20in.

[36] Ibid.

[37] Mayo Clinic. "Can Mindfulness Exercises Help Me?". Mayo Foundation for Medical Education and Research, 15 Sept. 2020. www.mayoclinic.org/healthy-lifestyle/consumer-health/in-depth/mindfulness-exercises/art-20046356.

[38] James Nestor. *Breath: The New Science of a Lost Art.* New York. Riverside Publishing. 2020

Printed in Great Britain
by Amazon

31752050R00130